The Stoic way of Life

The ultimate guide of Stoicism to make your everyday modern life Calm, Confident & Positive - Master the Art of Living, Emotional Resilience & Perseverance

Written By

Marcus Epictetus

Table of Content

Introduction

Do you find yourself often backing out from promises you made to yourself? These un-kept promises can be as little as missing the gym, putting your alarm on snooze, or the long-overdue laundry sitting on your chair to as big as procrastinating on the yearly goals. Do you feel like you cannot stick up for yourself? You want to say "no" at times but end up painfully agreeing to everything. Do you care too much about others' opinions of you?

If the answer is "yes" to any of these questions, then you are like one of the many troubled generations; emotionally weak. As hard as it may be to accept that, growth can only begin when you confess your lackings to yourself. If you really wish to turn a blind eye to all that may be wrong, let me assure you then that there will never be any room for growth.

No one is perfect, and it is completely alright to admit that. Remember, shame is deliberately staying stuck, not seeking an opportunity for growth.

There are aspects contributing to emotional weakness. They can be as natural as genetics to what environment you were exposed to and how you dealt with it. It even varies with age. Emotional resilience is empowering, and I can show you how to master it. Now to answer the question of "how," let me introduce you to a school of Hellenistic philosophy, Stoicism.

The wisdom of this ancient philosophy is eternal, and its significance is undeniable in the search for a peaceful and fulfilling life. The principle of "Stoicism" asserts that virtue (e.g., wisdom) is that pleasure and judgment are based on actions rather than words, and we cannot control and should not depend entirely on external events but on ourselves and our reactions. But it is a very basic, but not convenient, way of life at the very root of thinking. Take challenges in your life, and develop them into your asset, control what you can, and embrace what you cannot.

In fact, many of the great minds of history not only recognized it for what it actually was but they even practiced Stoicism: Walt Whitman, George Washington, Frederick the Great, Adam Smith, Eugène Delacroix, Immanuel Kant, Matthew Arnold, Thomas Jefferson, Ambrose Bierce, William Alexander Percy, Theodore Roosevelt, Ralph Waldo Emerson. Each of them reads the Stoics, learned, quoted, or admired them.

According to the famous modern-day scholar and essayist Nassim Nicholas, "A Stoic is someone who transforms pain into transformation, fear into prudence, desire into undertaking and mistakes into initiation."

About 304 BC, a trader named Zeno was shipwrecked on a trade mission. He had lost almost everything. Finding his way to Athens, the Megarian philosopher Stilpo and the Cynic philosopher Crates introduced him to philosophy, which changed his life, and he gave birth to Stoicism.

Stoicism allows us to embrace and get past whatever the tragic occurrences that arise in our lives. It is a true philosophy of healing. A Stoic never feels sorry for himself, nor does he cause his emotions to undermine his thinking ability.

Stoic ethics was focused on basic precepts that, even today, are still very powerful. Epictetus explained the meaning of deciding what depends on us and what does not: Our tendencies, our judgments, our dislikes, and our interests are what depend on us; in a nutshell, everything that is an operation of our mind. What do not rely on us are the money, body, awards, and high office positions meaning things that are not our minds' outputs.

When you do not worry about other people's opinions, you can waste less time and put that time to use focusing on your own self and goals. There is no point worrying if something does not depend on us. On the opposite, we need to resolve this grief, according to stoic logic. The entire stoic ethic is about the proper use of justification that, under all situations, we should allow us to be in command of our experiences.

There are three prominent stoic teachers after Zeno; the playwright and political counselor Seneca, the Roman Emperor Marcus Aurelius, and a slave Epictetus.

Seneca was a philosopher and also a self-proclaimed adherent of Stoicism. Of all ancient thinkers, one thing that really stood out from Seneca was that he was one of the most exciting and readable things. Much of that was attributed to the fact that in the medium of letters came his most notable works. We have two key tips for you to take with. Seneca wrote not only a collection of essays dealing with such realistic problems-adversity, mortality, and frustration, but also tranquility, leisure, and happiness. He also wrote about a variety of natural science topics-thunder and lightning, rivers, earthquakes, comets-and he created a considerable body of dramatic work.

Popular historians wrote that Marcus provided evidence of his learning not simply by language or comprehension of metaphysical doctrines but by his blameless nature and temperate way of life. He governed better than anyone else who was ever in any position of influence, in addition to having all the other virtues. Maybe the only text of its kind ever made is Marcus's Meditations. It is the personal views of the most influential man in the world counseling himself on how to make good on the obligations and roles and of his positions. It is the authoritative book on personal integrity, self-discipline, modesty, power, and self-actualization,

Epictetus was born trapped in slavery. His Enchiridion, which is described as a 'small textbook or a handbook', would be an ideal starting point for Epictetus. As it is filled with brief Stoic maxims and values, it is the ideal introduction to Epictetus. After formal teaching had ended for the day, Epictetus' discourses, found in Koine Greek, the ordinary contemporary version of the language, seem to document the interactions between Epictetus and his pupils. What we have in it is a series of personal but serious conversations in which Epictetus attempts to help his students carefully consider what a Stoic's intellectual life consists of and how to live it. He addresses a huge variety of subjects, from friendship to sickness, from anxiety to hunger, how tranquility can be gained and sustained, and why other people need not to be upset with one another.

This compelling and highly actionable book will show you how you can get on with life itself effectively. It is not very common that everything valuable and meaningful to us goes exactly the way we want it to, and that is life. You have to deal with it. Now it is your choice, you want to do that either feeling helpless or feeling empowered.

Though if you choose the latter, this book has been written for you. It will act as your mentor in achieving self-control, self-resilience, and calmness.

Continue reading this book if you simply wish to become the best possible version of yourself.

Chapter 1: Understanding the Philosophy of Stoicism

A brief definition of Stoicism would be that it is the philosophy of developing a logical and peaceful approach to one's life experiences and exposure concentrating on what lies in your control and putting aside what does not.

A prominent tutor of Stoicism became the secret diaries of one of Rome's greatest emperors, the intimate correspondence of one of Rome's finest playwrights and wisest power figures, the teachings of a former slave and exile. These remarkable records survive, against all odds, about two centuries later. They comprise some of the greatest insight in the world history and together form the basis of what is known as Stoicism, an ancient philosophy that was once one of the most prominent civic disciplines in the West, exercised in the pursuit of the Good Life by the strong and the weak, the wealthy and the oppressed alike.

The philosophical theory called Cynicism was created by Antisthenes, one of Socrates' pupils. He taught that virtue is the only good (living in harmony with our perfect disposition of unselfishness and reason; therefore righteousness, prudence, temperance, and power) and the opposite is only ill, and that we should therefore not be affected by any external thing. Therefore, his school determined that the most important thing a person should do is to prepare themselves very vigorously to be able to behave virtuously in all circumstances. This meant finding difficult conditions aggressively and being virtuous in them. The Cynics were deliberately behaving according to social standards, educating themselves, regardless of reputation, to do the right thing. We participated in askesis, or exercise, where they voluntarily exposed themselves to extreme physical environments in order to increase strength. Diogenes, the Dog, famously lived in an urn and possessed nothing but a cloak and a stick; they lived as moderately as they could, and trained sobriety. He used to own a cup, but when he realized he could use his hands to drink, he destroyed it.

A while down the road, a rich merchant, Zeno of Citium, was shipwrecked in Athens and ended up chasing the Cynic Crates. He practiced as a Cynic for a while. He took issue with their ignorance of physics and logic; however (they did not worry about anything but ethics) and thought that it was not mandatory though askesis was beneficial. Ultimately, however, he developed Stoicism, teaching similar ethics, but without askesis mandating, and also with the study of logic and physics.

Stoicism is either unknown or falsely interpreted, even for the most ardent seekers of knowledge. This vivid, action-oriented, and paradigm-shifting way of life has become slang for "emotionlessness" or the ordinary person. Provided that the mere mention of philosophy makes it most anxious or bored, "Stoic philosophy" on the surface sounds like the last thing someone would want to hear about, let alone in the course of everyday life desperately needs.

Stoicism is an instrument in the practice of perseverance, self-mastery, and knowledge in its proper place: something one uses to live a wonderful life, rather than an obscure area of intellectual inquiry. It would be difficult to find a term that dealt with greater oppression at the hands of the English language than 'Stoic.'

About 301 BC, Stoicism was a class of ancient philosophy founded by the Phoenician merchant Zeno of Citium in Athens. It was initially named Zenonism, but since Zeno and his disciples gathered in the Stoa Poikilê or Decorated Porch, it came to be known as Stoicism.

The Stoics gathered in public outdoors, on such porch, where everyone might listen to the conversation. You might argue that it was somehow a 'street ideology' for common citizens, not just aristocrats.

Stoicism was one of the most powerful and widely esteemed schools of thought from the outset and for nearly five centuries. It was one of the most prominent public disciplines in the West, exercised in search of the Good Life by the wealthy and the weak, the strong, and the suffering alike. But over the years, almost two millennia, the information that was once so important disappeared from view and was almost forgotten.

It was just after the 1970s that the influence of Stoicism rose again mainly because it was the intellectual inspiration for Cognitive Behavioral Therapy (CBT) and because of the theory penned by writers such as William Irvine and Ryan Holiday.

Hopefully, the historical background of Stoicism has been quite clear by now. Now let's discuss the core principles and virtues of Stoicism.

1.1 Virtues of Stoicism

In Stoic theory, there are four essential values. According to the pioneer of Stoicism, Marcus Aurelius, if we are to come across something better than truth, righteousness, bravery, and self-control, it must also be something remarkable. It was almost 20 years ago. Since then, humans have discovered a lot of things, cars, the Internet, treatments for diseases that were once a death sentence, but have we discovered anything better?

Have we found anything better than being courageous?

Have we found anything better than moderation and sobriety?

Have we found anything better than doing what is right?

Have we found anything better than truth and understanding?

No, we have not. It is doubtful that we will ever. All we encounter in life is a chance to relate to these four characteristics. So, let's talk about justice, courage, temperance, and wisdom:

- **Justice**

The most widely admired value by the Stoics is doing the right thing. There is no other more significant Stoic virtue than justice, for all are influenced by it. Marcus Aurelius himself considered justice to be the root of all the other virtues. Throughout history, Stoics have pushed and promoted justice, always a huge personal risk, and with great bravery, in order to do great things and protect the people and ideas they cherished.

There are numerous activists and leaders who have taken to Stoicism to gird them against the challenge of struggling for the values that counted, to lead them in a world of so much wrong to what was right. A Stoic wants to assume profoundly that a person can make a difference. Effective advocacy and political maneuvering need awareness and planning, as well as realism and optimism. Wisdom, recognition, and also a refusal to recognize the status quo are necessary.

- **Courage**

Seneca would say that he genuinely pitied people who had never suffered tragedy before. He said that no one would truly know what you are made of and capable of, not even you. You have gone through life without an enemy.

The universe needs to decide what group to put you in, which is why it will sometimes send you to your way complicated circumstances. Think about them not as inconveniences or tragedies, rather as options, as responses to concerns. Am I courageous? Am I going to face, or run away from, this problem? Am I going to stand up or get turned over?

Let your acts respond to the record and let them reassure you that the most important thing is courage.

- **Temperance**

Life is not, of course, so plain as to suggest that bravery is all that matters. While all will admit that bravery is necessary, we are all well aware of individuals whose bravery transforms into recklessness, and when they begin to risk themselves and others, it becomes a fault.

It is here where Aristotle comes in. In his famous "Golden Mean" metaphor, Aristotle simply used bravery as the main example. He said that there was cowardice at one end of the continuum, which is a lack of courage. There was recklessness, on the other hand, so much bravery. What was asked for was a golden mean. What we needed then was the proper quantity.

Temperance or moderation is about doing nothing in abundance. It is all about doing what is right in the right amount in the correct way. Since we are, in fact, what we repeatedly do, excellence is, therefore, a habit, not an act.

Virtue and quality is a way of life, in other words. It's basic. It's like an operating system, and habit is the code that this system runs on.

As Epictetus would later conclude that power is proven and develops in its subsequent actions, walking by walking, and, moreover, running by running. So, if you want to do anything, make a habit of it. So, if we want to be successful, if we want to excel, if we want to be amazing, we need to develop the skill we need to develop the everyday habits that allow this to happen.

This is terrific news. And it suggests that, without herculean initiative or mystical recipes, remarkable effects or enormous improvements are possible. Small changes, good processes, the proper procedures-these are the things that it takes.

- **Wisdom**

Temperance. Righteousness. These are life's critical values. What circumstances, therefore, call for courage? What is the amount that is right? What is the thing that's right? This is where it comes to the last and necessary virtue: wisdom, awareness, and learning; the experience needed for the environment to be navigated.

The Stoics have long valued wisdom. Zeno said that one mouth and two ears were given to us for a reason: to listen more than to talk. And because we have two eyes, we have a responsibility to learn and observe rather than we say.

In the modern days, just as it was in the ancient world, it is important to be able to differentiate between the massive clusters of information at your disposal and the true wisdom you need to live a decent life. It is vital that we learn that we keep our minds open forever.

Epictetus said that you could not understand what you believed you already knew. That is real.

This is why we not only have to be humble scholars, but we also need to strive for great teachers. That is why we should be reading at all times. That is why we should not avoid practicing. That is why we have to be vigilant in filtering the signal out of the chaos.

The aim is not only to collect knowledge but the right kind of knowledge. These are the teachings contained in Meditations, from the real Epictetus to the entrance of James Stockdale into the realm of Epictetus. These are the main details you need to absorb, breaking up from the background noise.

The universe has thousands of years of burning wisdom at its hands. You are likely to have the power at your side to discover everything you desire. So today, by calming down, being intentional, and seeking the wisdom you need, respect the Stoic virtue of wisdom.

These four virtues are fundamental to Stoicism.

1.2 Core Beliefs of Stoicism

There are many principles of Stoicism. To get a better understanding of the essence of Stoicism, let's move on to the core principles it dictates:

- **Agreement with Nature**

  The essential purpose of life was decided to be Eudemonia by all ancient schools of philosophy.

  Eudemonia, this life objective, is a little difficult to interpret. Think of it as human beings' ultimate happiness or satisfaction attainable—a lofty, flourishing, and smoothly flowing life: The Good Life.

  To advance to the Good Life, the Stoics came up with several realistic tactics.

  A human being is a logical animal. That is what distinguishes humans from sheep and beasts. We are unique, both for better and worse, from all the other animals on planet Earth. The point of concern is not that we have different skin, smaller teeth, or thinner bones, but our social and mental skills.

Our potential for reasoning is what differentiates humans from all other animals. Since doing so negates our dignity, the most valuable and natural thing we have, we do not live like sheep or beasts.

Living in harmony with nature is about behaving like a human being rationally instead of like a beast arbitrarily (and out of passion). In other words, in all our acts, we can still apply our innate capacity to 'reason'. If we use logic, we live in peace with nature, so we behave as people are expected to behave. Humans are supposed to use rationality to act as humans, not as animals.

- **Focusing on the Control-able**

Allow the full use of what is in your control and, when it happens, take the rest. Some things depend on us, and some things do not depend on us. Epictetus just mentioned this philosophy at the beginning of his writing, Enchiridion. This idea is central to the stoic philosophy and doctrines of Epictetus. The most distinctive theory of Stoicism is essentially this so-called 'Stoic dichotomy of control.'

We have to differentiate carefully between what 'is up to us,' or under our own control, and what is not. Our voluntary decisions, including our acts and judgments, are up to us, while everything else is not within our influence.

For example, our bodies are not up to us, or at least not entirely. I think there are many things I can do to have a safe and desirable body. But this is only to a certain degree feasible. I can control my behavior and eat a balanced, high-fat diet, systematically workout and walk a lot, but I have little control over other aspects, such as my genes, my early exposure and interactions, and other environmental causes, such as diseases and accidents.

I monitor only my own actions, and I have to acknowledge with equanimity the result. By truly knowing that I am doing my best and doing everything in my power to get where I want to be, I get my happiness and trust. So, either I can accept the outcome easily because I know I did my best, or I cannot because I know secretly that I did not do my best.

This is a huge morale builder in my mind. To fulfill your tasks, you do everything you can and everything that is beyond your control. And then you happily head through the moment of reality, when you have done your very best. If the result is not satisfactory, you will simply embrace it and say, 'Well, I did my very best.'

You can reflect on what you can control and acknowledge what you cannot. You know that you have not done your best, or you have not acted appropriately when you feel the need to justify yourself.

The most important things about life are the things that are up to you, your emotions, and your actions. The most attractive part of Stoicism is that we are responsible for our growth because we are responsible for all that really matters in life. So, the biggest thing to take away here is to direct our energy and where we have the most strength and then allow the world to take care of the rest.

- **Living by Virtue**

What the Stoics meant by 'virtue' in terms of our logical human existence was excellent or thriving. Basically, you are enjoying the Good Life because you live according to virtue. In various types of virtue, this individual perfection takes place, or, simply put, we will excel in various ways. The Stoics listed these numerous types of virtues as the four cardinal virtues that we have discussed above.

Today, as you live according to these values, you are moving towards the true purpose of creation, the Good Life, or Eudemonia. So, the perfection of purpose and behaving according to virtue, or being 'virtuous,' is the secret to behaving the Good Life.

And if you uphold all the virtues, would you be noble in the Stoic sense. For starters, if you behave bravely during the day and then get drunk at night, you are not genuinely noble (because with all the binge drinking, you violate the virtue of self-discipline). Virtue is a kit for all-or-nothing.

It was obvious to the Stoics that virtue would be a reward of its own. You do something, you do because that's the right thing to do. For your own sake, you behave in harmony with God, with reason, and according to the cardinal virtues. It does not matter what you get out of it because as you move into the Good Life, doing according to righteousness is satisfying in itself.

Again, the word 'virtue' really refers to excelling with one's own personality and applying reason in a safe and praiseworthy way.

- **Good vs. Bad vs. Indifferent**

The Stoics distinguished between things that were 'good',' evil' and 'indifferent'.

Justice, wisdom, bravery, and self-discipline are the cardinal virtues of good things. The inverse to these virtues is the negative ones, including the four vices to cruelty, folly, indulgence, and cowardice.

All the rest, but mostly life and death, glory and bad reputation, riches and hardship, enjoyment and suffering, and health and illness, are indifferent things. Indifferent things like fitness, wealth, and prestige can be summed up.

In short: The Good Life is absolutely oblivious to oblivious things such as fitness, prosperity, and prestige. Simply, they do not exist. They are neutral. If you are wealthy or poor, good or ill, the overall happiness does not matter. We should then learn to be 'indifferent to indifferent things' and learn to be content with everything nature puts on our plates.

Indifference does not imply coldness. On the opposite, because indifferent objects are not up to us, someone greater than us desires them, and we get to love them equally.

Although indifferent objects may not be 'good' in fact, some are nevertheless more desirable and superior to others. Therefore, the Stoics classified indifferent things from 'preferred' and 'dis-preferred.'

A rather rational view was taken by the Stoics. Indifferent beneficial things such as good health, fellowship, money, and good looks were listed as favored indifferents, while dispreferred were their opposites.

The Stoics, however, made harmonious, eudemonic life an attainable objective for all, regardless of social class, fitness, education, or appearance. While all of these virtues are preferred, they are also insensitive to leading a virtuous existence and are not necessary.

People will always choose pleasure over suffering, prosperity over hardship, and good health over illness, so go ahead and look for those things, but your dignity and living in harmony with virtue is not threatened by doing so. In other words, it is easier to suffer sorrows, poverty, or illness in a noble way than to achieve pleasure, riches, or health in a shameful one.

- **Taking Action**

Even though the Stoics regarded external things as indifferent, their own actions were not at all indifferent to them. They had to try to do the 'right thing,' and the Stoics had to behave in harmony with morality to get to the eudemonic world. The Stoics were the doers.

Stoicism is a very practical philosophy of living. It is not enough for the Stoics to learn about how to live a life of their own, but to really go out into the world and practice their ideas. By doing the right actions, you would earn the Good Life.

You should not be content with studying abstract thoughts on how to live your life, but you must apply those thoughts aggressively. Knowledge and information, if not implemented, are cheap and worthless.

- **Reverse Clause**

As Stoic learners, we are supposed to do the right thing and do our hardest to get there, but with equanimity, we are also supposed to embrace the result. Do the very utmost to excel and realize and understand equally that the end consequence is beyond the direct control. We develop a strategy and do everything to fulfill our objective, but we realize at the same time that something can happen and deter us from completing our objective. We accept that and change our approach to the new situation, and aim to do the best we can again.

As starters, in sports, you concentrate on the process, you concentrate on the commitment, the planning, the training, and everything in your control, and you take the outcomes as they come. Being the best player and doing the best you can, is the main objective, not the winning.

- **Practicing Misfortune**

The concept of adversity premeditation is to envision potentially "evil" situations repeatedly beforehand so that they do not take you by surprise, and you will be able to face them peacefully and behave according to virtue.

No matter how disastrous a scenario might seem, those external circumstances are neither good nor evil for the Stoics, nor indifferent. It is just our responses that can be positive or evil. So, get your mind prepared and introduce yourself by creativity to tough scenarios, and in real-life situations, you will be safer and less vulnerable.

- **Loving the Undesired**

The Stoics encourage us to genuinely enjoy what has happened, whatever it is, instead of merely embracing what happens. It is a bit unnatural to have a love for something that we never wanted to occur. Think about a higher force that turns the globe and rules on everything that happens. And all incidents happen directly to you, whether desired or unexpected. It can feel wrong at the moment when something happens, but it serves something bigger that you do not yet understand, which will eventually help and benefit you.

- **Making Opportunities**

It is all about how we understand what happens around us and what we determine what those events mean. How we understand the universe and how we perceive what is happening to us make a gigantic change in the way we live our lives. This makes your life accountable to you. External events are not controlled by you, but you control how you want to look at them and then react to them. And, that is all what counts, in the end. The secret to recognizing these possibilities lies in your interpretation. It is much more important how you see things than the things themselves. In all, you will see the positive. Stoicism encourages one to think of anything as a chance for progress. This encourages one to turn everything, challenges and gifts alike, into opportunistic causes.

- **Mindfulness**

Mindfulness is a requirement for the practice of Stoicism, but it is often strengthened further through practice. It functions in both directions. Again, being attentive is about being alert enough to take a step back from your own feelings and then being able to select the right action instead of working on autopilot.

When you witness an emotion, you need to know that you feel that emotion at the exact moment; only then you can determine whether or not the feeling is beneficial and what the best reaction is. If you do not realize that you are behaving out of emotion, choosing and modifying your actions is incredibly difficult.

These ten core principles of Stoicism encompass the roots and basics of this school of thought. Let me introduce you to some famous philosophers of Stoicism in the next section.

1.3 Philosophers of Stoicism

Stoicism can do wonders for mankind. Without flinching, self-mastery and inner determination make it possible for Stoics to go through exceedingly adverse situations, all the time trying to behave rationally and logically. The keen understanding of the unpredictability of the universe and of the briefness of life is at the heart of Stoicism. Stoics, however, are not willing to spend time and resources on futile discussions or initiatives. The transition of negative thoughts into a sense of perspective prepares us to have the ideal state of mind at work and in our personal lives to make the right choices.

The ancient Stoic philosophers come from nearly every perspective imaginable. One was a slave, the other a king. One was a carrier of water. The other was a popular playwright. Some were traders. Others were independently affluent. Some of them were senators, and some of them were soldiers. The philosophy which they taught was what they all had in common. They concentrated not on the external world but on what was entirely in their own influence, whether they were leading the Roman army or chafing under the shackles of slavery: their own feelings, their own acts, their beliefs.

Marcus Aurelius served as the Roman Emperor for almost two decades. The gravity of that place and the degree of influence Marcus possessed is necessary to remember. At the moment, he occupied the world's most influential role. Nothing would be off-limits if he wanted to. There was nobody who could restrain him from all of his urges. He could indulge and submit to temptations. There is an explanation of why the saying that power has become a cliché throughout the history of absolute corrupt. And yet he proved himself worthy of the position he was in.

Seneca, who was born in southern Spain over 2000 years ago and was raised in Rome, is the second most influential Stoic in history. Seneca was an influence on prominent figures such as Francis Bacon, Pascal Erasmus, and Montaigne. For men and women in action, Seneca's Letters from a Stoic are a must read, providing timeless metaphysical wisdom on riches, sorrow, faith, strength, and life.

What makes researching Stoicism interesting is that in terms of where they stood in society, three of the most well-known practitioners varied extensively. One of the world's most powerful positions was occupied by Marcus Aurelius, the emperor of the Roman Empire. Seneca was an emperor's adviser, a famous playwright, and one of the Roman Empire's wealthiest citizens. And then there's Epictetus, on the other hand, who was born a slave. This is what makes Stoicism so powerful: it can have timeless virtues to assist us in both good and poor fortune, regardless of our position in life. For decades, his work inspired the masses and was even accepted as the central ideology by Emperor Marcus Aurelius.

This chapter covers the essential fundamentals of Stoicism, and in the next chapter, we will discuss that Stoicism is not just an old philosophy, it is a contemporary philosophy and how you can apply Stoicism to the modern world.

Chapter 2: Stoicism in the 21st Century

Stoicism is a way of life, not just some ancient theory restricted to dusty philosophy books. You cannot get away from it. It would even remain applicable in the hundred years to come because it speaks to our feelings and emotions, which are the true essence of the human soul.

Now I will guide you through the journey of Stoicism in a nutshell before we move onto its relevance to the modern-day world.

2.1 Journey of Stoicism

The ultimate purpose of our lives is eudemonia for stoics: a state of prosperity and contentment that can be accomplished by living in line with nature. Existing with nature involves both serving your purpose in the world and existing as a human being (which is very closely linked to conceptions of destiny and providence). Since human beings, through their capacity to use reason, separate themselves in essence of their existence from all living beings, they should behave according to their justification. We have to behave rationally, in short, and not allow our emotions fool us. There are neither positive nor negative external conditions, but it is better that we are oblivious to them. Over thousands of years, this purpose of eudaimonia i.e. contentment and growth and the methods of reaching it have been established.

Let's have a brief description of the golden age of Stoicism. It is the period, which starts from 300 BC and ends in 200 AD. This golden period is typically split into three parts: the early, the middle, and the late stoa. The last one is better known, as only sources still present are from that time. Let's get into it:

- **300 BC – 100 BC**

About 300 BC in Athens, Zeno of Citium founded the school of thought Stoicism. He rejected the famous school of thought Epicurism, put forward by Epicurus, who, motivated by pain and pleasure, inclined towards a materialistic universe and an unintended existence. From (among others) the teachings of Cynicism, which prioritizes simplicity and virtue, Zeno established his school of Stoicism. At the Stoa Poikile in the middle of Athens, he began teaching. It was covered, freely available colonnade that produced the name of his school of thought: Stoicism. The cornerstone of Stoicism was laid by Zeno, and the school had an immense influence. In three areas: logic, physics, and ethics, he developed a distinction in stoic philosophy. Most focus is on ethics now, even though the founder Zeno would argue the idea that logic and physics must support ethics.

Zeno was replaced by Cleanthes, his pupil, who largely adopted Zeno's teachings and incorporated a bit of his own. Chrysippus of Soli was the third chief (scholar) of the school stoicism. The three pieces of philosophy were greatly developed by him, most known by creating a framework of propositional logic. Chrysippus maintained the status of Stoicism as one of the greatest philosophies of all time by extending and solidifying the groundwork laid by Zeno. After him, Diogenes of Babylon, Zeno of Tarsus, and Antipater of Tarsus led the academy.

- **100 BC- 1 AD.**

The prominence of Stoicism began to move to Rhodes and Rome from Athens, beginning about 100 BC. The seventh scholar, Panaetius, was a lot more pragmatic than the stern Zeno in his views. He found stoic theories about physics easier and was a lot less concerned with logic. This moved the philosophy of Stoicism closer and more accessible to Neo-Platonism. He introduced Rome to Stoicism as well. Panaetius is known to be the last scholar, owing to the more extensive and diverse existence of the middle stoa, accompanied by variations of opinion. A united and undisputed philosophy of Stoicism was no longer available, but stoic school of thought would prove to be able to survive the challenging test of time.

Posidonius re-ensured Panaetius' theories and got even closer to Aristotle and Plato. In Rome, Stoicism was embraced by Cato The Younger and Cicero. It is particularly possible to view Cato, famous for his inflexible moral honesty and his strict way of life, as a sign of Stoicism. He appears more closely identified with Chrysippus and Zeno's traditionalist doctrines than with Posidonius and Panaetius' diverse philosophy.

- **1 AD – 200 AD**

The main field of concern for stoic philosophers in the Roman Imperial era was ethics. Physics and logic have not been investigated as much anymore. Two hundred years long late stoa, since it is the sole time period from which full original writings are still in existence, is the best-known time of Stoicism. One of these texts comes from Seneca, who, in his Moral Letters to Lucilius, used real day-to-day events to address moral problems. He is highly admired for his own writing style, and he still reads his Epistulae today. For his

Discourses and Enchiridion, which were issued by his student Arrian, another stoic philosopher, Epictetus, is known. The Handbook of Epictetus is a decent start if you are searching for an introduction to Stoicism. Though Epictetus was born into slavery, Marcus Aurelius emperor of Rome was probably the most famous Stoic. Ta eis heauton, which he initially wrote as a private diary during his military operations in Germany, is his most influential work. That is now widely referred to as Meditation. "Meditations" is perhaps the stoic work that is most debated and read and still provides inspiration for a better life to people today around the world. In our contemporary age, notions like reason, self-discipline, age, and citizenship are still important concepts. Meditations by Aurelius are still seen as a means of personal growth and development and have aroused renewed attention in recent years.

These were the three prominent periods of the growth of Stoicism. Now let's understand how Stoicism can still be practiced in the modern era.

2.2 Modern Day Stoicism

Stoicism has been around for an extensive period of time, and for quite a while, its penetration into Western thought has been happening. The stoic theory has inspired poets, theorists, and politicians over the centuries and indirectly weaved it into many Western thinkers' works.

There are many Facebook groups on Stoicism. The biggest of which has more than 25 000 participants as of 2017, and the Stoicism Subreddit (2017) has over 54,000 subscribers. There are email lists on which fierce disputes rage over points of theoretical detail: various Stoic blogs, some Stoic advisors, and hundreds of videos on YouTube.

There is a "Traditional Stoicism" website that has broken away from the other "new" communities on the basis of an insistence that devotion to ancient Stoic physics and theology is needed to live according to Stoic ethics.

There are the "Modern Stoicism" and "How to be a Stoic" email feeds, in which posts are written every single day on Stoic facts, texts, and topics, and, in the latter case, a common Stoic Advice column.

In comparison to, or as a corollary to, Stoic beliefs, some organizations propose Eastern meditative beliefs to "mindfulness."

Then there is a website "Daily Stoic" that sends email addresses to subscribers' daily Stoic meditation themes: whether quotations from the great Hellenistic and Roman Stoics or from literary and metaphysical works on Stoic themes. For many causes, Stoicism, though, has made a surprising apparent re-emergence:

- **Socialization Structures Failure**

There were structures in several years past that could be counted on by an individual to help him make sense of life. The church, the classrooms, and the family unit were some of these. Many of these systems have been significantly weakened in our current society and/or are no longer as important.

Many individuals do not really go to church, schools cannot compete with the Internet, and single parents are the heads of many households.

You have a future where the next day is different from the previous, leading to the fact that the digital world produces tidal landscapes of transition. People are looking to the perennial essence of secular Stoicism for guidance to find a grounding in this turbulent universe.

- **Massive Accessible Information**

In just one week, more information is produced than was produced in the first several thousand years of human existence. Ideas circle across the globe so quickly that one can catch on and grow viral extremely rapidly.

Stoicism speaks to the people because everybody wants to improve himself. They just want to be stronger. Everyone wants more sense of self. People want their lives to be more in their control. On all of these, Stoicism provides a simple prescription. You can add that to the fact that every year there are many fantastic books and websites on Stoicism and modern Stoicism published and launched. You have the easy accessibility to the contents of ancient philosophy with several loads of them.

- **Undeniable Advice**

In all times, stoic wisdom extends to everyone everywhere. This is the concept of a "perennial philosophy." Human nature, no matter what tradition or place of origin it comes from, will still be human nature. In addition to witnessing the vastness that life has to offer, Stoicism at its heart reflects on how to cope with human existence (other people's and your own). It is very enticing.

The significance relies on a few very basic assumptions and concepts that are powerfully intuitive.

These begin with the clear call of Epictetus to individuals to always differentiate between what is not and what is in our power. There is no logical argument, at any fundamental stage, of being disappointed with the things we cannot change. To reflect on what we can influence, learning to let go of these things, our own current desires, emotions, and acts, just need to be both philosophically astute and a therapeutic boon.

Imagine that all people with mental energy invest thinking about what others think about them, tweet about them, do not like, or say or do not say about them. What may happen in the future or maybe even not, and what cannot be changed in the past, would be freed up to attend only to the things that can be changed at present.

This way of thinking will get you close to what the Stoics pledge, through their (Socratic) emphasis that the inner character (virtue) of individuals is the most valuable thing that anyone may reward or seek,

All of the other external aspects are "indifferent" to the Stoics, from prestige to fame to influence wealth to anything open to the adverse factors of outrageous fortune.

That is, they are neither good nor evil in themselves, nor does their possession or loss "make us" happy or sad. It is our opinions of objects that confer this influence over us upon them. Except by argument, certain decisions may be contested and reframed by experience and determination.

Stoicism has recently been reported as one of the best "mind hacks" ever invented, in today's words. Despite the destruction of their towns, houses, and loss of acquaintances or even loved ones, the resultant advertised capacity of Stoic "sages" to be able to hold up "philosophically" has earned the school the perennial image of being joyless, "grin and bear it" affair.

However, in order to achieve inner harmony, the Stoics do not wish or require individuals to sacrifice anything. Instead, Stoicism asks citizens to cultivate internal capital in order to be equanimity able to cope with success and hardship.

Stoicism has remained one of the permanent threads out of which Western culture has been woven, from the Serenity

Prayer to Roosevelt to Shakespeare to contemporary writers such as Tom Wolfe or Walt Whitman.

And while most of us can find certain features of international Stoic physics and theology, there appears to be nothing about this ethic that is or will ever be ancient. Until today's 21st century renaissance in the banner of Stoicism, this realization prompted the pioneers of Cognitive Behavioral Therapy to incorporate Stoic concepts and recommendations into 20th-century psychotherapy.

By reading the above-mentioned reasons and justifications, I am sure you have understood that Stoicism is very much relatable and applicable in the present. There are many famous modern time personalities who follow Stoicism, and some even preach it. Let me get you through them one by one briefly.

Revival of Stoicism

While the influence of Stoic teachings during the Middle Ages was primarily limited to solving problems of social and political importance, it persisted for the Renaissance to provide the foundations for the resurgence of Stoic views in epistemology, logic, and metaphysics, as well as the recording of the more common Stoic theory, in its zeal for the rediscovery of Roman and Greek antiquity. There are many philosophers who brought the light back to Stoicism like Justus Lipsius, Giordano Bruno, Pietro Pomponazzi, Huldrych Zwingli, Blaise Pascal, Benedict de Spinoza, etc.

I have jotted down below some personalities who followed Stoicism in their path to success, and I am sure you will be surprised by many of the names:

- **Bill Gates**

Bill Gates followed the message of staying humble if we want to learn and succeed. Epictetus is, of all the Stoics, the nearest to a real teacher. He had a classroom. He had classes hosted. In reality, through a student who has taken very good lecture notes, his wisdom is handed on to us. One of the aspects that irritated Epictetus about students of philosophy, and irritated all college professors throughout history, is how students pretend to want to be educated but really secretly assume they know it all already. In today's upcoming entrepreneurs, you see this regularly: arrogance mixed with a lack of modesty before the eventual collapse.

The truth is, most of them are guilty of believing that we know best, and if we put that mentality down, we would all understand more. There is always someone who is better, is more successful, improved, and wiser than we are, as clever or successful as we can be.

Ralph Waldo Emerson, the writer of the 19th century, put it well that any man he encounters is his master at some stage. In some of the most popular market executives, we occasionally see this style of mindset. They are humble and seek suggestions actively and learn from everyone they know. Sam Walton, Walmart's founder, suggested that we should learn from everyone.

You also see that in Bill Gates, Microsoft's co-founder and philanthropist, a voracious reader who every day wants to learn the world a little bit, one book at a time. It is a humbling reminder of just how little you know, even though you are one of the most famous business magnates in the history, to continually open yourself to new insights and ideas.

- **Elon Musk**

Elon Musk followed the message of nothing to make anything just out habit. An employee is asked, "Why did you do things this way?" The response is, "because it's the way we have always done things." This reaction frustrates any successful employer. The employee has stopped thinking and is working out of habit mindlessly. Any logical boss will ask the worker to leave.

Can you agree that this is the mindset of a hyper-successful entrepreneur like Elon Musk? Not, of course! As he said that it is the best piece of advice to think endlessly about how you can do it differently and challenge yourself.

To our own working practices, we should add the same ruthlessness. In reality, to crack the rote behavior, we should research philosophy specifically. Out of memory or habit, find what you do and ask yourself: is this really the right way to do it? Understand why you do what you do. Do it for the correct reasons.

- **Pete Carroll**

Pete Caroll follows the message of turning failures into opportunities. Seattle Seahawks coach, Pete Carroll, is legendarily positive and also an understudy of Stoicism. Throughout his career, his coaching methods are focused on finding the inner grit of himself and his players, and taking on the supposed negative things that have happened and turning them into positive things. Carroll took the Super Bowl XLIX loss and onslaught of abuse over his final decision costing the Seahawks the game and pressed on into a new year. This is what the Stoics are doing.

- **Warren Buffett**

Warren Buffet follows the message of living below means. Warren Buffett, who basically has a net worth of about $85 billion, lives in the same house he purchased for $31,500 in 1958. A lineman for the Baltimore Ravens, John Urschel makes millions but manages to live on $25,000 (2017) a year. Also, with a deal worth some $94 million, Spurs star of San Antonio, Kawhi Leonard, gets around in the same 1997 Chevy Tahoe, he had, since he was a teenager. It is not that they are poor. It's because the stuff that matters to them is cheap.

Buffett, Urschel, and Leonard did not end up this way by mere chance. Their way of life is the product of prioritizing. They cultivate interests that are obviously beyond their financial means and, as a consequence, any revenue will give them the freedom to do the things they care the most about. It just happens that, beyond any expectation, they became rich.

In the universe, this kind of insight is what they love the most, which means that they will enjoy their lives. And if the markets were to switch or their lives were cut short by an injury, that means they would still be pleased.

A strategy understood by many business leaders is to live below your means. Amazon was deliberately designed by Jeff Bezos with a culture of frugality. According to him, he believes just as other constraints do, frugality fuels creativity. Inventing your way out is one of the few ways to break out of a small cage.

Mark Cuban, a billionaire businessman, has also promoted the ruthless reduction of unnecessary spending: The more you stress payments, the tougher it is to concentrate on your goals. The better you will work, the greater your choices.

Many of the palace furnishings were famously sold by Marcus Aurelius to pay off his empire's debt. He did not need luxuries, and they weighed him and his people down.

The more things we seek, and the more we have to do to earn or protect those accomplishments, the less our lives are truly valued and the less secure we are.

Let's get onto some daily life practicality of Stoicism.

Modern World Problems – Ancient World Solutions

Stoicism is, at its core, a philosophy of minimizing your life's negative emotions and enhancing your joy and gratitude; it includes rituals of mindfulness and living based on value. Stoicism, both externally and internally, is a method to amplify the human experience. I have put together some modern daily Stoicism life practices for you to follow:

- **Happiness Triangle**

The happiness triangle has three main elements, as mentioned below:

Eudaimonia, the fundamental purpose of existence agreed to by all ancient philosophies, is at the center of the triangle. This is the greatest promise of Stoic philosophy, and it is about leading a supremely peaceful and smoothly flowing life. In our lives, it is about thriving. Essentially, that is what we all desire, to prosper and live happier lives, right? This is why it is at the center of the Triangle of Stoic Happiness. Do you recall the word's Greek origin? It means being with your inner daimon, your supreme self, on good terms (eu). And how can we accomplish that? Through living with Areté.

Each-moment, express your ultimate self. We need to seal the gap between what we are capable of and what we actually do if we want to be on great terms with our highest self. Actually, this is about being your best version of the here and now. It is about using reason and working in accordance with profound ideals in our behavior. Obviously, this is better said than achieved, and what helps this optimistic aim is to distinguish good from evil and rely on what we manage. Concentrate on What You Control: In Stoicism, this is the most influential theory. We ought to reflect on the items we manage at all times and take the rest as it arises. It is necessary to accept what is already because it is beyond our power to undo it. Ultimately, what is beyond our power is not essential for our flourishing. What is important for our wellbeing is what we want to do with the external conditions provided. So, it is always within our power, no matter the situation, to try to make the best of it, and to live with our ideal self in harmony.

Taking responsibility is the last element. Good and bad come exclusively from yourself. This continues the first two corners that say external factors do not matter for the good life, so it is enough to succeed in life to survive with areté, which is beyond your reach. Often, because of any external incident you do not control provides an environment you do control, including how you want to react to this incident; you are responsible for your life. In Stoicism, this is crucial; it is not events that make us happy or sad, but our understanding of such events. The day you choose to allow outside circumstances no more control over you, this is when a tower of strength will be born.

- **Avoiding Materialism**

It appears like our consumerist culture creates more appetite than it satisfies. Our relentless media and commercial consumption leave us wanting and finding better out there, wasting our hard-earned dollars on the new fad, being assured that it would leave us happy before next year's arrival of version 2.0. Our appetite reduces as we tend to want less, and we become more content with what we have.

- **Be Genuinely Content**

You may have realized by now that satisfaction comes from inside and from appreciating everything around us, including something as basic as living at the moment in time where we can buy bottled water from a vending machine no more than 200 feet from us for $1.00 (sometimes we really take it for granted). Because our satisfaction will become independent of other influences with the stoic mentality, we can be satisfied as stoics all the time, and we want nothing more than human experience. We could cause ourselves to be frustrated if we wished for more. This does not suggest that stoics do not appreciate the better things of life; it just implies that we do not think of them for our pleasure as well. It can only leave us completely content by bringing goodness to the world by supporting others and advancing humanity, which we can do on a daily basis.

- **Picture the "What If"**

We have now learned that desire for having more leads to unhappiness, but how do we find happiness? In gratitude, the key lies. Everything that we have, we have to respect and take satisfaction in it. With convenient access to essentials and innovations, we live in an unprecedented time of history that offers a quality of life that was unforeseeable just a few decades earlier. We take this for granted instead of appreciating it. One of the stoic traditions is to consider sacrificing any of your prized belongings. It can initially sound depressing, but we come to understand what we have more by imagining these defeats. It is important that we do not put too much value on the things we have because they may not always be there. When you put emphasis on an external thing, and it is stripped away, the stoic may not be frustrated but more thankful that they have the thing, to begin with. Becoming a Stoic involves seeking satisfaction in everything you have. Anything from the cosmos is borrowed. Materials come and go, but there remains goodness, and joy lies therein.

These are some of the basic stoic practices you can incorporate in your life to make yourself more in control of who you are and stay content. Thus happy.

Chapter 3 – Modern Day Stoic Practices

We all realize deep down that there is something that we can do and be. Indeed, much guilt comes from recognizing that a certain situation could have been dealt differently than we did. We freak out over the minimal on our children and then torture ourselves for days after with shame over it. We have a project deadline due at school, and we procrastinate on it before we have no choice but to pull an all-nighter, the whole time we get it done, feeling nothing but pressure. None of this is new; for practically thousands of years, humans have been putting off things they have to do, obsessing about things beyond their grasp, and giving in to counterproductive emotions.

All of us even seem to get more reflective at the beginning of the year. We begin to reflect on how the year ended, where we are now, and how much we have improved or not. We dwell on what should have been done differently, how we have treated people, and what we have left undone. We make resolutions based on these reflections. We resolve that we are going to stop smoking or start working out, starting next year. The new year begins, and soon, sadly, we give in and return to our old ways at the first sign of trouble. We light the cigarette, we lash out at our wives, and we continue to suffer the bad feelings associated with ourselves being frustrated.

This is not to say that it is trivial to uphold all of these measures, but it does not alter the fact that it has to be achieved. The argument is that the practice of self-improvement is continuous, and the possibility for practice is everywhere. And it is not worth losing these chances. Here are a few Stoic practices that, no matter where you come from or what the conditions are, will support you all in every facet of your lives:

- **Stoic Acceptance**

    Stoic acceptance is about recognizing what is beyond one's influence instead of what is. Human brains are vulnerable to agonizing about the past or the future. We will waste hours ruminating about incidents that are entirely fictitious. We need to establish an internal locus of control. Any of what exists in life is not within our influence. This undeniable reality was known by the Stoics, and so they concentrated on what they could do.

    Born a slave, it would appear like there was no justification for Epictetus to think that he could control everything. He was severely crippled by a fractured leg his master had given him. Epictetus survived all hardships with grace.

Epictetus would argue that his thoughts, interests, and aversions still remained his, even though his property and even his body were not under his power. That was something he was in control of.

Nowadays, it is easy to get irritated. We are so used to comforts and amenities that even the smallest inconvenience triggers indignation within us. The normal instinct is frustration, if not anger, if the internet takes a moment longer than it should or if traffic stops for a minute.

It is not any of these breakdowns that make us dissatisfied. The dissatisfaction stems from the emotional response that we have chosen. The responsibility is on ourselves to ensure that our inner state of mind is not affected by the external events. Once we internalize that, it becomes clear that, regardless of our conditions, we have the power to be happy.

It is all about self-acceptance and self-honor. You have to tame your mind.

The worst betrayal a person can do to himself is to make his mind feel that he has lost his composure. And the only thing that you can do about yourself is to behave like a survivor while you can be a fighter. Do not be dominated by your emotions. Let your inner strength empower you to be fully alive.

If you are not a part of this game, then it might be tough for you to cope with the harsh realities of life. People are going to intervene, challenge your choices; they are going to flood you with all sorts of views. Maybe they will also convince you to become just like them. Do not just fall into that trap. Stay raw; stay true, because that makes you who you are.

We are not part of a competition, nor are we doing a marathon because we have got to keep an eye on the winning trophy. Keep yourself cool. Do not let the rat-race mess with your happiness.

You will understand that nothing is more crucial than your mental health once you lose your calm. Take time if you need some time to bounce back to life; take sufficient time to know which direction to go.

Not everyone has the same collection of goals, dislikes, or likes. So instead of hating the work or finding yourself in a certain place trapped. Making the best of what you do and making it your goal.

Just make peace with your mind, for not every person has the same life view. Therefore, to some, what luxury is for you can be ludicrous. Similarly, it might not be someone else's cup of tea to find satisfaction in the easiest stuff. You need to know that and respect the decisions of others.

Do not ask others to like what you like, as they will begin to dislike you. Instead of seeking to influence others, they only cherish their individuality. We, humans, are beings that are complicated. But the truth is, there are people like us who think like us and have stories to share in the same way.

If you desire to sit alone and enjoy it, so it is completely fine. If you find happiness in solitude and 20 people like to be in a group, then chase solitude. Do not drive yourself in a certain direction just because others want you to do it. It will generate total confusion, and you might end up hating everything.

- **Time Misers**

All the intellectuals of history, according to Seneca, could never truly articulate their perplexity in the corruptness of the human mind. The slightest disagreement with a neighbor will mean hell to pay or even a foot of their estate, no person can give up, and but we quickly let others enter our lives. Worse than that we happily pave the way for others who would later command our lives. No one hands his money out to passersby. In opposition to that how many of us have handed out our lives to others! With money and property, we are tight-fisted, but think so little about wasting time. It is the one thing that we should all be the toughest guardians of.

There will be countless interruptions every day: calls, guests, emails, and unforeseen incidents. Booker Washington noted that the people who are willing to consume one's time with no reason are almost innumerable. On the contrary, a philosopher understands that these violations hamper us from doing the contemplation and work that we were supposed to do as our purpose on earth. This is why they defend their feelings and personal space so diligently against trespassers and vulnerable neighbors. They understand that more than any conference or article, a few minutes of reflection are more worthy. They also realize how meager time we are currently given in life and it is very easily possible to deplete our stocks.

It was the death of a friend who made businessman and entrepreneur Tim Ferriss realize that it is surprising that we waste time concentrating on the insignificant individuals who add little but their selfishness. We have to stop this and instead concentrate and abolish distractions, one of the best business minds from the last century, as Peter Drucker, put it that push yourself to set goals. If you cherish the thought that you have got time for everything, you are going to end up doing loads of affairs you do not have to do indulge yourself in.

We are reminded by the Stoic teacher Seneca that we may be good at defending our physical property, but we are far laxer at upholding our mental limits. It is possible to reclaim property; some of it still untouched by man. Time, however? Time is the most irreplaceable resource; instead of attempting to make the most of it, we should actually avoid spending too much of it so easily.

- **Defeating Fear**

There are many ways to negotiate and mitigate the effects of anxiety, but Stoicism provides one of the clearest ways to deal with your fear by trying to push through what you fear most-an essential heuristic for life where it is even more dangerous to postpone decisions out of fear of failure than to make a risky decision.

The ancient stoics continually reminded themselves and their followers that all of us are mortal and have only a short time to have an impact on the world. Instead of denying, facing the fear of death head-on and accepting, it allowed the Stoics to be braver and more productive in their daily lives.

Seneca wrote that, as if we were coming to the very end of life, we must prepare our minds. Do not let us postpone anything. Every day, let us balance life's books. There is never a short time for those who put the final touches on their lives every day.

You will be more efficient and never run out of time to achieve your goals and tasks by having to confront the fear of death, Seneca suggests. Seneca writes for people who fail to encounter their fears that life is very short. If you continually put off action out of anxiety and fear, you cannot accomplish your objectives. Challenging your fears is the first step to achieving the goals you set.

In contemplating death and confronting their worst fears, ancient philosophers are not the first ones who have found value. CEOs such as Steve Jobs and Jeff Bezos are also taking a stoic approach to putting their fears in the light of personal or business mortality.

Steve Jobs gave a starting speech at Stanford in 2005 in which he addressed how focusing on his own mortality enabled him to conquer his fears of failure. Jobs said that remembering that he is going to be dead soon is the most important instrument he has ever encountered to help me make life's big choices. Because of almost all of these things, all social aspirations, all dignity, all fear of humiliation or defeat, just fall away in the face of death, leaving just what is really necessary.

In order to survive, Jobs had to take on tremendous pressure as the CEO and founder of Apple and create wildly ambitious goods. Jobs relied on the old stoic tradition of considering his death to help bring those fears into context in order to alleviate his fears that these goods and programs would fail. The consequences of errors and mistakes at Apple did not appear as serious or alarming in the light of imminent death. As a result, without being overwhelmed or hampered by fear of disappointment, Jobs was able to concentrate on completing projects.

To brace themselves for defeat, the Stoics used times of harmony and stability.

- **Going Beyond Pleasure**

Stoics advocate voluntary suffering as a greater effort to recognize the positive stuff in one's life. Depriving yourself briefly of things that offer comfort to your life. Without really knowing (e.g., personal car), items that you can quickly become dependent on. Voluntary pain is a simulation of the imminent future, in addition to reminding you of the good stuff in your life, where unexpected events can strip you of the security once considered a norm.

Pleasure comes with a sign of alarm as well. Although happiness is not intrinsically incorrect, the dark side of happiness is often followed by remorse or other kinds of regret. Therefore, if you use cost analysis to treat your impulses for enjoyment, you might understand that forgoing enjoyment creates more pleasure if you weigh in the price of the satisfaction of will-power and guilt.

You are required to put in a lot of time and work to embody Stoicism, which means you will always encounter contradicting influences on the path to Stoicism; the Stoic ideals you adhere to and your actual actions. Although this is natural, in order to escape frustration, it sits helpful not to confuse Stoic values for your identity. Alternatively, you are advised to establish a stoic spectator.

Your Stoic observer will evaluate and monitor success in your Stoic conduct. The product of Stoic meditation is this inner contact. Stoics examine emotions and previous behavior in order to learn about them, as compared to Buddhist meditation, where you have to let go of your emotions.

Stoic behavior is not intended to be visible. The characteristic of a beginner is to brag about your Stoic principles; true Stoics do not stand out.

One of the most prominent concerns that Stoicism beginners have is, "What luxuries can I avoid?" In fact, they wish to know if, in search of a happier life, stuff like video gaming, gambling, alcohol, and the stuff like this can be avoided. This is a valid issue, but it is the incorrect one, eventually. Stoicism is not about stripping yourself of all you love, contrary to what others may claim. It is not about seeing a mesmerizing sculpture or painting as the colorless mass, or refusing to go out with your friends or eating a delicious meal and tasting nothing.

No, happiness was not seen by the Stoics as anything to be deprived of. If a happy life is the goal, then we need to understand how and when preference, definitely a big element of pleasure, fits into the bigger picture. In accordance with the Stoic conception, the purpose that pleasure plays in life is that it must follow goodness. Without goodness, the pleasures of life are false pits. They are able to make you reliant on their continuous existence and to enslave you. Life becomes impossible without these joys, leaving you despondent and helpless.

Stoicism is all about providing you with the mental and emotional armor that life inevitably puts you through to protect yourself against the highs and lows. It gives you the assets by which both pleasure and pain can be experienced because if you have not trained yourself to manage them properly, both can lead to ruin. When pleasure is brought into the discussion, in the words of Diogenes Laertius, a well-tamed mind would be able to see pleasure as "indifferent." That is part of the Stoic practitioner's work: to recognize that there is ephemeral enjoyment and pain. What you enjoy can be stripped from you or even used against you.

One thing you do not realize, however, is that Stoic theory has the ability to transform culture and extends way beyond its self-help applications, which only make up just a limited portion of its capacity.

Its simplicity is the essence of Stoicism. It does not make you oblivious to it, despite its demand for indifference towards social status, material goods, and the harsh language of others. Evidently, even the shallowest analysis of the words of Marcus Aurelius is adequate to alter your perceptions, aspirations, and place in the universe. Fear, pain, agony, and misery lose their hold on you, while your ego ceases to be fed by social media exposure and professional accolades. The influence is liberating: as one refuses to dwell on oneself, the energies of the mind are unleashed to follow morality.

For Stoics, life is based on the progression of goodness through goodness alone, embodied as the only true good, righteousness, knowledge, bravery, and self-control. Simply stated, the Stoic pursuits are not prosperity, fitness, prestige, and the possession of material goods. It simply means that everyone may be rich but unhappy. Equally, education, by itself, is not a quality, specifically because deprivation, inevitability, and environmental oppression would be generated by a poor one (where sin is propagated, not necessarily where the standard is dubious). Therefore, the balance of inner isolation and external empathy, and as we note in our open access article, the expression of selfishness by selflessness, is a proper Stoic activity, as Massimo Pigliucci nicely sums up.

Obedience to the Stoic virtues clearly lends itself to a more balanced workplace, school system, and culture in general. The mutual decision to work for self-control, fairness, bravery, and intelligence then feeds off personal change or deterioration. When you imagine a society where the Stoic evils of cowardice, inequality, hypocrisy, and greed rise high and facts are respected less than the presumed importance of the person who utters a hollow counter-argument, this becomes clearer.

We should not believe that it is expected, or appropriate, for a Stoic to treat everyone the same way. In fact, the notion of "circles" of consideration was explored by ancient Stoics like Cicero and Hierocles to express the belief that we instinctively feel a more direct bond with friends and family than we do with others. We must understand, though, that the belief that we both belong to and engage in a cosmopolitan culture of mutual common citizenship is an important characteristic of Stoic philosophy. In particular, Hierocles emphasized the notion that we should put inward circles of consideration to represent the healthier facets of humanity that represent the self and role of self in humanity. This Stoicism, in doing so, provides the basis for a culture that is founded on unity rather than populism.

Stoicism, in this sense, teaches that "obstacle is the path" is not only private it is also a common call to overcome the obstacle together. Now, take a minute to focus on the ability you have to bring change by your investments, including the food in your freezer, the car in your driveway, and the clothing on your back before you find out that social challenges are beyond your grasp. All this stuff means something about you; basically, where you put your dollar or peso is an indication of your beliefs.

You understand that it is your legal duty to challenge the fundamental presumption that it is immediately in your best interest to add (a) and (b) to your possession as you wish to strive towards the Stoic virtue of justice. Whether things (and not virtues) are favored indifferents, at best, (a) and (b), as long as getting them does not become a barrier to your progression towards virtue and (maybe) strengthens your life. At worse, (a) and (b) weaken the road to righteousness when you buy into the systems that produced them by buying them: questionable work conditions in Asian sweatshops and computer factories, the devastation of the South American rainforest, or shady banking transactions in London and New York. That does not infer that the elimination of capitalism is asked for by Stoicism. Indeed, for the Stoics, any dogmatic devotion to capitalism or Marxism, or any unwavering allegiance to the philosophy of the left or right-wing, irrespective of the essence of the views articulated, is unreasonable. This is because there is no political wing of reason or logical thinking, and facts belong to everybody.

- **New Beginnings**

Start living at once, and count each day as a separate life. The Stoics saw possibilities brimming with every day. Know, to fully alter the course of your life requires just a single occurrence, a single conversation.

A bad day does not have to turn into a horrible week. If the fire of anger is not put out, failure to reach a deadline will expand to a rejected business proposal. Where required, the Stoics constructed walls of internal compartmentalization. Small bits in the big picture bind and impact each other. When cancer of rage and negativity is detected, before it grows, it has to be taken out. A blank slate, a fresh day. Before your little failures turn into a big problem, put a halt to the domino effect.

- **Embracing Your Distress**

The Stoics were not unfamiliar with pain like everyone else has walked this planet. It was just as much a part of life in Rome as it is today. The reign of Marcus Aurelius, though the people of Rome loved him, was anything but simple. Civil revolts, wars, pandemics, and financial crises all tested his strength. It would be a preposterous understatement to say that Epictetus suffered early in life: the first three decades were spent in harsh, grinding slavery. He will eternally wear the scars of it.

When their lives took abrupt twists, even the more recent Stoics, including James Stockdale and Viktor

Frankl, were both compelled to embody Stoicism. They have suffered much like you are suffering. They battled, just like now you are struggling.

That is because life is not fair. And it is complicated.

But what was unique about the Stoics was that they continued to glow precisely in these tough moments. It was from this hardship that immense importance stemmed from them. James Stockdale spent seven years in a miserable prisoner of war camp. He said that he believed not only that he would get out but also that in the end, he would triumph and turn the experience into my life's defining case, which he would not trade in retrospect.

Crises make us care just about ourselves, how we are hurt, what we are trying to do to survive. But realizing that the whole planet is witnessing the same thing is vital. Marcus gives himself (and us) in Book Six of Meditations in order to keep an important thought in mind. He wrote that frequently meditate on the interconnectedness and reciprocal interdependence of all things in the world. He talks of Sympatheia's Stoic principle, the notion that all things are interwoven together and thus have an affinity with each other. We are meant to support each other and be kind to each other. Sympatheia can supply us with sense when it looks like it is falling apart.

It is unfortunate because, once it is no longer in our hands, so many of us refuse to truly understand the impotance of anything. We all take under-appreciate what we have and desperately crave what we do not have. Even Viktor Frankl, who endured horrific massacres in Dachau and Auschwitz for three years, admitted that he, too, took the small stuff for granted. It is the little stuff in difficult times that gives one the sense required to keep working.

We are all guilty of dwelling more on what we need rather than what we do have in times of hardship. Instead of expressing gratitude for the stuff we have not missed yet, we whine. Remember to put your energies into helping people the next time you feel overwhelmed by the state of misery. Do not forget to be happy with what you have. In everything, seek beauty.

- **Strict Honesty**

According to Epicurus, the first step to salvation is an awareness of wrongdoing. There is no urge to be made right for a person who is not conscious that he is doing something wrong. Before you can reform, you have to catch yourself doing it. Show your own remorse, conduct investigations on your own into all the facts against yourself to the best of your abilities. In mitigation, play the first part of the lawyer, then of the judge, and ultimately of the pleader. At times, be rough on yourself.

When you are not sure of why you did not finish your job today and decided to watch Netflix instead, it is hard to change habits.

The urges that prevent us from turning up, participating, committing, and being present are crucial to be aware of. Ask yourself why you feel this way. Get to the bottom of it. Investigate it. Use it as a cue to go ahead anytime you feel resistance. Of course, the trick is teaching yourself to think that way.

It is not a matter of ability or any unconscious reflex. The cultivation of self-awareness of how you think, feel, and respond is a muscle to think through your thoughts. The more you use it, the more it gets better.

These are some of the many stoic practices I will present at your disposal in the next chapters.

Chapter 4 – All the Way to Emotional Resiliency

Stoicism can teach you to get rid of emotional weakness. Remember, your body is an extension of your soul, and Stoicism offers growth of the soul. The theory of Stoic was an invaluable help to the Romans and Greeks, who both lived in a society that was especially brutal in many respects. It is an ancient theory that can be crucial even today, helping you manage the confusion and noise of the world in which we live. Here are some ways Stoicism offers you emotional resilience:

- **Stoic Meditation**

    In the Eastern context, the classic Stoic texts do not usually apply to meditation-that is, as a complete relaxation of one's mind. Classic Stoic meditation is something like a clear-thinking practice.

    Clear thinking suggests that one strives to conceive the situations only as they are in the ups and downs of life. Instead of excessively optimistic rose-colored glasses, or unnecessarily pessimistic dark ones, one sees things as if through transparent eyes.

Marcus Aurelius writes in his Meditations about being faced by life's clouds or disturbances. They may be big or small. On the road, are there hurdles? Go around them then. Do not ask, 'Why do these things exist?' Although contributing little to one's satisfaction, such investigations or value decisions only disturb the peace of mind.

Many of the events of existence, of course, are more potentially distressing than hurdles in the road. Aurelius takes a more complicated situation into consideration: you hear that someone is chatting behind your back. It is better to take things at face value from the Stoic viewpoint of Aurelius: sure, everybody is talking about you. But it would not help the peace of mind to speculate further about what precisely the entity is saying, or if this might make them a bad guy, etc.

You should not jump to conclusions like a Stoic or react to anything you hear or see. If you feel that learning more is necessary, you can always ask the individual what they have been talking about you and why. But you might still conclude that it is not worth the hassle and that you would not let your peace of mind shake anyone else's view of you.

Aurelius and other Stoics insisted that it was not the circumstances of life that irritated them. Rather, it is our judgment or assessment of circumstances that worries us, the intricate stories we tell ourselves about encounters. It is not because they pain you, but your own opinion of them, whether you are pained by external things, and it is beyond your power to blot out that opinion now.

In the same way, Epictetus could argue that a human could be in danger and yet happy, sick, and yet happy, dying, and yet happy "by a Stoic mental framing of events.

For the Stoics, the only sanctuary is a well-controlled mind or spirit. Aurelius says in writing about how people often want to get away from it all, to the beach, to the country, to the mountains. You can get away from it whenever you want by going inside. Nowhere you can go to is quieter than your own soul.

Therefore, Stoicism holds that while we cannot always govern events, we can always govern how we think of them. And how we think of them is going to decide whether or not we stay at peace, and therefore happy and prosperous. Cognitive-Behavioral Counseling (CBT) for many years has expected this focus on how we think about situations and how this impacts our feelings and behavior.

In CBT, it is often assumed that how we learn of problems can be regulated and modified. The CBT approach to depression, for instance, holds that negative symptoms (such as intense and enduring sorrow) are at least partially due to the suicidal perception of a maladaptive story we tell ourselves about our lives or situations.

It is often assumed that our feelings about a particular occurrence can be re-shaped or "cognitively restructured," and therefore become less stressed about it. Reflecting on one's death is one Stoic reflection that deserves special notice. This is believed to help us place the ups and downs of life in the right light and to inspire us to make the most use of whatever time we might have.

Let your mortality decide what you do and what you say and think.

In his conversations with the Indian magician Don Juan Matus, Carlos Castaneda wrote a feeling of a memento mori. Don Juan advises Carlos in his Trip to Ixtlan that Death is the only wise counselor we have. This suggests that dreaming about one's eventual demise helps to bring the circumstances about life into perspective and shows what is really important to oneself.

Here are a few meditations that have been put together for you:

1. **A View from Above:** Marcus Aurelius encourages us to do a 'view from above' exercise. This practice allows one to envisage oneself from the third person perspective. In this experience, though keeping ourselves in the center, we zoom out. We continue to zoom out and ponder the universe's size e.g. your first zoom could involve a view of you from above your house's roof. Increase the magnitude, and you can see your street view, increase the magnitude, and you can see your country's view. Keep going before a glimpse of earth from the stars can be imagined.

Through this view, we will achieve a clearer understanding of the insignificance of our concerns. Whatever problems we might find extremely insignificant relative to the cosmos. When we put things in context, it is much easier to conquer the emotional challenges we face.

2. **Voluntary Discomfort:** Epictetus told us of this exercise. We are going to intentionally put ourselves into stressful conditions in this exercise. In order to prepare ourselves to not cling onto comfort with too great regard, we will do this. Voluntary pain can be carried out in a variety of ways. Some tips are:

   o Exercise in the morning
   o Hot Showers
   o Fasting for one day
   o Walking without a sweater in the winter
   o Slumbering on the floor

Your relationship with ease will change all these things. Life can get much simpler if you resolve the need for warmth. It will be much better to set the targets and adhere to them. This technique is going to harden you up for good.

3. **Negative Visualization:** Despite the term, negative visualization is an activity that, if done regularly, will

improve the default level of satisfaction. The practice consists of you thinking what it would be like if you lost certain things in your life. Any of the things during the workout that you might think are:

o   How it feels to lose your social standing.

o   How not to have a roof over your head would feel.

o   How it would be to live in a country in the third world.

o   How it would feel for a loved one to suffer.

o   How it would be to have a physical handicap.

The aim of this exercise is not to be gloomy or morbid; it is to put things in perspective. Allowing you to see how genuinely lucky you are. It also trains you for situations in the worst condition in which one of these things occurs. You are not supposed to dwell on these ideas, but from time to time, remember them.

Naturally, as you accept items being withdrawn from your life, you tend to develop a sense of appreciation. This is a very realistic way for you to exercise appreciation. Gratitude is necessary now because of a thing called 'hedonic adaptation'; literally, it is a concept that describes the propensity for people to often return to their default happiness level.

Your base level of satisfaction will grow for a while if you win the lotto and become a millionaire. However, you can revert to your base stage as you get used to the lifestyle, amid all the expensive gadgets. Gratitude breaks this cycle, causing each step up the ladder to be celebrated. When you own a box, you can be grateful, and when you own a Lamborghini, you can be grateful.

- **Avoid Impossible Hope**

  The Stoics would not advise you to cheer up or be cheerful if you are down because life gets tough. You have never been told to be more optimistic.

  They were simply propagating the reverse.

  They believed that you were not supposed to have hope for the future, but rather eliminate hope. To the stoics, the heroin of feelings was hope-the higher you are raised, the lower you fell.

  Stoics also warn you that horrible stuff is going to happen. Your vehicle might get stolen, you might go to prison, but it is going to be all right. They are trying to tell you your life is full of misfortune and that you are going to get through everything. They claimed that the result of incorrect decisions is negative emotions. That our expectations of life are false and that we needed to behave in compliance with life.

A healthy mental state, for the stoics, is determined by its potential for reason and goodness. A unanimous conviction in the stoic culture is that emotion should not motivate us only logic and reason. This does not mean absolutely stamping out the feelings.

It means getting the thoughts out of the driver's seat and putting them in the passenger seat. The belief in living in harmony with nature is perhaps problematic in our hedonistic modernity. This suggests that food is solely for life, and wellbeing and sex is just for reproduction.

They thought you might end up being possessed by the ownership of material goods. Buying more things can only add to the fear that these things will be preserved.

Their conviction in suicide is perhaps more divisive. They thought a man should be able to take his own life. In fact, when his student, and now Emperor Nero, asked Seneca to commit suicide, he did not bat an eye. As his wife and children hold onto him weeping, he declared confidently, why is the need to cry over parts of life? All of life calls for tears.

- **Accepting Fate**

Friedrich Nietzsche popularized the idea of embracing one 's destiny around 1882 when he invented the Latin word, Amor fati. The theory, however, goes back farther, and the Stoics, thoroughly realizing what was and was not within their influence, made embracing one 's destiny or Amor fati, a cornerstone of their philosophy.

Epictetus uses the example of a bath to explain embracing one 's destiny in the Enchiridion, curated by his pupil Arrian:

When you take some initiative, remind yourself of the purpose of the initiative. If you are trying to bathe, imagine the things that normally happen in the bathroom: some people spill water, some kick, and some use abusive words. Thus, if you say to yourself, "I will now go bathe and keep my own consciousness in a state consistent with nature," and in the same way with respect to any other action, you will go through this action more comfortably. For, therefore, if some difficulty emerges in bathing, you would have it ready to say, it was not only to bathe that you needed but to keep your mind in a nature-conforming state; and if you are troubled with things that happen, you will not keep it.

The Dichotomy of Power, which is the Stoic tenet of knowing what is and is not under one's power, is part of this notion of embracing one 's destiny. The objects beyond our influence, Epictetus thought, are:

o   Pursuit
o   Opinions
o   Aversion
o   Desire
o   Our own acts

Things claimed by Epictetus were not under our influence are:

o   Property
o   Body
o   Command
o   Reputation
o   Whatever our own acts are not

Therefore, fate is not something in our hands, and it contains components of existence that we have only "partial" hands over; that is what the Stoics categorized as "not being in our control."

Among the other Stoics, Marcus realized that he was in control of himself, of his actions, and of his effect on the world. But other than that, the universe itself and the actions of others have no influence over him. Therefore, while writing in book two of Meditations, he places himself to take advantage of his situation.

It is now time to understand the essence of the world of which you belong, and to the governing force to which you are the offspring; and to understand that your time does have a limit to it. Then use it to progress your enlightenment; else, it will vanish and never again be in your power.

Marcus reminds himself of the influence he has inside himself, that his time on earth is restricted, but that he is a part of a much greater image regardless of what he does and pursues, over which he actually does not have complete control.

During the times of the Stoics, embracing one 's destiny was important, as many of the Stoics whose works endure today, such as Epictetus, Seneca, and Musonius Rufus, preached philosophy under emperors who were decisive in their assessments and made cut-second decisions that caused the intellectual community to reverberate. At some point in their hard life, each of the above-named intellectuals finds himself exiled.

Emperor Claudius banished Seneca from Rome in 41 AD.

Epictetus, banished by Emperor Domitian from Rome.

Musonius Rufus, like all intellectuals of the time, was banished from Rome in 71 AD by Emperor Vespasian.

All three had to let go of their lives and travel, giving up everything that they had, including their right to live the life that they wanted to live.

They reminded themselves to be present at the moment and to embrace the life-given events.

- **Momento Mori**

As this phenomenon is briefly described above, just think of yourself as dead. Your life has been lived by you. Take what is left now to live it properly. The legend goes that a star-struck crowd will be cheered on after a famous battle general walking triumphantly through ancient Rome. With the general saying the words 'Memento mori'-which translates as remember thou art mortal -a slave will walk side by side.

For a second, think about it. How different everything would be if someone else muttered 'you're going to die' every time we were told how wonderful we would be in a sales pitch? Or while we count the likes of our selfies? Or when a long-overdue promotion is awarded? When we are continually reminded of our mortality, how much more modest and graceful we can walk through life.

The thought that we could die too is pretty depressing for all of us. It makes us mad about our humanity. But instead of saying that life is too short, listen to one of the fathers of Stoicism, Seneca, who said:

"Life, if you know how to use it, is long."

The Stoics knew that it was an essential road to happiness to come to terms with death, rather than being defined by it. We should then use our impending mortality as the driving philosophy, giving it a sense of intent and priority, to live a more fulfilling and fruitful existence.

And if you ever think about death, note that a long time before you were born, you were dead. Back then, it was not all that bad, was it?

- **Premeditatio malorum**

As this phenomenon is briefly described above, Premeditatio malorum advises you to constantly watch out for what could go wrong, roughly translated as prepare for all evils. It is a pessimistic lesson in imagination that forces you to imagine everything that could go south. It is outstanding as a mental tool, and it trains you for the many challenges of life.

But you do not have to shut yourself off from what could be considered as negative consequences in order to actually live a healthy life and become happy, whatever the concept of success is.

And while planning for the worse cannot do anything to modify the worse, your endurance is educated. You will be much more able to cope with them as difficult situations arise. Premeditatio malorum helps you to keep your nerve instead of being blown off track by circumstances when you have already agreed on the path ahead beforehand.

With those who know about Cognitive Behavioral Therapy (CBT), this notion about planning for the worse will ring a bell. Indeed, CBT therapists frequently encourage their clients to constantly imagine fearful occurrences as if they had already occurred as part of a strategy called mental habituation. Clients become more successful in controlling their fear and think less about the future by teaching them to confront certain events in a controlled way.

It is an alarming sign. It may be delusional to only wish for the future, but it is also catastrophic and too much pessimistic thought. A stoical approach to loving your destiny allows you to look at all angles at events and performance, both positive and negative. Then, the general position becomes that of neutrality.

Ryan Holiday neatly puts it as expecting a fun filled and fruitful day. Be ready just in case it is not.

- **The Obstacle is the Way**

Stoicism encourages one to accept and respond to hardship with a feeling of lightness and even cheerfulness.

In reality, in spite of the morbid touch, the Stoics are quite a positive group. They assume that any negative has an equivalent and the opposite, flipping the concept of premeditatio malorum on its head. Any negative is, therefore, a positive.

We should accept challenges according to Stoic teachings and see them as chances to exercise some of the Stoic virtues of justice, charity, religion, hope, courage, temperance, and prudence.

They inspire us, not in spite of what's before us, but because of it, to treat any drama as an opportunity to succeed. By wanting less, by letting go of all the foolish assumptions you have accumulated in your self-absorbed existence, by forgetting about happiness and realizing that anything important in this universe needs hardship and compromise, you will live a more rewarding and meaningful life.

Of course, we are humans. So, even as we want to turn up as our best selves in our decision-making, some unreasonable impulses will probably play havoc. By holding our thoughts in balance and being steady, the best way to fight is this point of view.

That does not mean throwing aside negative thoughts and emotions or dismissing them. Our thoughts, on the contrary, are an important part of who we are, and we do not wish to be apathetic or neglect our capacity to feel anything.

Instead, Stoics advocate equanimity-calmness and patience that helps you to balance yourself and not panic. It is a sense of poise that keeps you from being blinded by passion. You lose the anchor and become anchored instead of being swept up by the wind. You then ask yourself: Does panicking bring something positive to this situation at this moment?

Historian

Ada Palmer speaks about the development of an inner fortress as if she sees her concentrating on something that upsets me, and she has a kind of triage of reactions. She asks herself (A) Is it possible to find an actionable answer to the issue? If not (B), will she get me to stop worrying and let go of the issue? Is it possible for her to ask herself if this would matter in a year or five years?

Challenges are nothing more than an ability to exercise some virtue like persistence, modesty, bravery, resourcefulness, fairness, reason, and imagination. The three disciplines are dependent on each other.

1. **Persistence:** It is how we see and realize what is going on around us, and what those events would mean is what we decide — a root of power or of great weakness, maybe our expectations. We only add to our problems if we are subjective, emotional, and short-sighted. We must, as the ancient people practiced, learn how to limit our impulses and their influence over our lives in order to avoid being consumed by the world around us. To swat away the parasites of bad expectations, to distinguish accurate messages from false ones, to root out bias, anticipation, and anxiety requires discipline

talent. But it is worth it because the reality is what is left. While others are scared or excited, we will keep calm and undisturbed. Straightforwardly and simply, we will see things as they actually are, neither good nor evil. In the fight against challenges, this would be an enormous advantage for us.

2. **Action:** Action is commonplace; appropriate action is not. It is not any kind of conduct, as a discipline, that can do, but guided conduct. In the service of the whole, everything must be completed. We will dismantle the barriers in front of our step by step, action by action. We will behave in the best interest of our priorities with persistence and versatility. Action requires bravery, imaginative application, not brashness, and not brute strength. Our movements and choices characterize us: with boldness, deliberation, and determination, we must be sure to act. Such are the virtues of correct and good conduct: nothing more, no feeling, avoidance, or assistance from others. Action is the solution to our predicaments and the cure.

3. **Will:** Will is our inner force, which the outer world can never influence. It is our last card for a trump. If action is what we rely on when we still have some agency in our situation, when the agency has all but gone, the will is

what we rely on. Placed in a situation that appears and undeniably and unchangeable destructive, we should turn it into an experience of growth, a humbling experience, and an ability to provide others with warmth. That is the strength of will. Yet it must be cultivated. Even in dark days, we must brace for hardship and chaos, master the art of acquiescence, and cultivate cheerfulness. People too much believe that, that is how awful we want anything to be. In fact, with defeat, the will has much more to do than with power. True will is quiet strength, modesty, and flexibility. Weakness masked by ambition and bluster is the other type of will.

- **Eradicate Ego**

  Modesty is the secret to achievement, but to know that some deity-awful people are doing well in life, you do not have to go too hard.

  The ego can be a strong but unreliable driver of success. It will caress you on a good day, whispering that you are invincible and better than anyone else. It would bury you with pain on a bad day.

  Stoicism acknowledges that when it comes to being popular, having a big ego will also be useful. But it also admits that by sacrificing your character and your spirit, you pay the price.

Stoics claim, close to Buddhists, the ego reveals itself as an exaggerated sense of self-importance. It keeps us from possessing the modesty to realize that we know only a limited proportion of what we need to know. This keeps us from learning.

It is what the popular rich ones know most deep down but find it hard to accept that we are not as incredible as we think we are. We applaud ourselves for becoming the room's smartest individual. Alternatively, we should be wondering why we were too frightened to associate ourselves in the first place with more knowledgeable individuals.

Ryan Holiday puts it as the ego is the enemy of what you desire and have: the supremacy of art of working for others well, of true imaginative insight, of building loyalty and assistance, of lifespan, of repeating your performance and sustaining it. This discourages incentives and prospects. This is a magnet for rivals and failures.

As author James Clear said that the surest way to keep yourself from knowing a subject is to assume that you know it already.

These stoic practices will help you become mentally strong by keeping your emotions under control and have a logical approach towards everyday problem-solving.

Chapter 5 – Get Rid of Stress, Trauma, Fear & Anger

When I said Stoicism is a way of life, I meant it. It is not something philosophical you will read in this book and forget in a week as you find no relevance of it in your life. It is the cure to the obstacles that impede you in living a healthy and happy life. Stoicism holds the key to solving real-life problems like stress, trauma, fear, anger, and greed. These issues of the mind will not let you have a peaceful life to fulfill your purpose of birth. I have put together the ways to deal with all of these problems and even disabilities. You will know, the body is an extension of your soul. You need to purify your soul to have a purified bodily experience. Let's get started:

5.1 Stoic Ways of Getting Out of Stress

In our lives, we all have stressors. They are so many or so strong at times that they can seem daunting. So, if you would like your life to be better, that is fully understandable. But the wish is vain at the same time. What life throws at you, you cannot control. You will not avoid stressors from invading your life, no matter what you do.

However, all you should do is determine how you want to view them. Wisely and rationally, you can opt to respond to the stressors. And you can learn in the end how to survive even in the face of uncertainty.

When we look at what constitutes "stress," we discover that it is an undue, exaggerated, or inappropriate response to a situation. Not only can stress have detrimental consequences on the psyche, but it also affects our physical wellbeing and may contribute to decreased effectiveness, disability, and occasionally death.

It is extremely crucial that we continue to assess our lives to see where we are, with the understanding that possible health conditions exist and can be triggered by stress. Are we late with regarding certain payments? Are our present relationships impacting our mental clarity? Are our unnecessary obligations wearing us down?

Here are a few ways to get rid of stress:

1. **Creating a Gratitude List:** Gratitude is believed to raise our "feel-good" hormones in the body. Not only does our whole day shift as we write what we are thankful for, but by seeing the benefits of our lives, we are able to truly understand the people and things

around us. This trains the mind to actively seek what is beneficial, thus reducing the level of stress.

2. **Keeping Anxiety Down:** You may be worried about what you have done, what you have not done, or what you ought to do. It could be a previous 'failure,' a poor interview, relationship, public humiliation, or worse yet some sort of physical or emotional violence. While always letting it hurt you, you might be 'running away' from the past. Yet the distinction of those that are under our power and other those that are not under our power is one of the core concepts of Stoicism. Nothing from the past you can change. Will you have power over stuff that has happened already? Of course, the answer is no.

We then have to embrace the experience happily and refuse to let it have any effect on us now. What is done is in the past. We only have so many resources and effort to draw in a day, so why waste it on the uncontrollable events? These ideas of the past are also just impressions; these impressions are not facts; they need not to be viewed as such.

What Seneca was talking about is the extraordinary opportunity we have to decouple our cognition as human beings. Decoupled Cognition is our capacity to reflect on something that has occurred or will occur while also remaining mindful of our surroundings. It also covers our desire, within our own minds, to have a dynamic relationship with another human (even an abstract one) at another time and location. We may also place ourselves "inside others," wondering what they think and how they will react to us. We can see how valuable this talent is for social engagement and planning, but it is also the root of all our woes.

We have come to be in a constant state of decoupled cognition-in the current moment, never ever being. How much do we really immerse ourselves either in the past or the future in activities at hand without 'one eye'? How much do we have discussions with people while not even listening or moving the car, and don't even remember the journey until we get to our destination? Typically, this loss of understanding is because we are so busy being worried about the past/future or upset or hankering that we do not really realize what it truly is like to be present, just-be.

No man limits his sadness to the present. If we are continuously trying to get the attention to the present moment, our mindfulness will increase; unhappiness and fear will be difficult to take control over us.

The future lies within the domain of things we cannot control, as, in the past, things are not under our' power.' It makes us understand how pointless it is to spend some time thinking or dreaming about it, clearly making us realize that the future is indeed uncertain. Hope and fear are the same. Both of them are the 'enemy of the present moment,' and we should always understand that any enemy of the present moment is our enemy.

It is clear how it can make one nervous about dreading the future at the moment, but optimism is even more complex, more cunning in the way it can create uncertainty and trigger unhappiness. Hoping for the future leads one to wish things to unfold in a certain manner and, therefore, to live a life in contrast to amor fati. It is also this wish and optimism that truly leads us to fear over those effects, triggering our anxiety. Remember, Amor fati and consider doing what you can for what you have right now and survive at the moment.

3. **Distinguishing Pain and Suffering:** Pain is a part of life that is inevitable. Suffering is voluntary, though. The initial reaction that you have to a hurtful incident is pain. Suffering is what happens when you contribute to the suffering in your imagination.

   For example, assume that you have broken your leg. Your discomfort stems from tissue that is hurt. Your suffering is the result of your thoughts about pain. "This agony is bad. What if it does not ever go away? Perhaps I will never ever be able to walk properly? Anxious thoughts like these can add your pain to a tremendous amount of suffering.

   So, pay heed to the mind's plot. Do not forget that thoughts are not facts. And it is within the power to choose whether or not to trust them. And it is within the power to choose whether or not to trust them. Yes, you are in agony, but all that you really know is that only needless misery will be added to build stories of what the agony could cause.

I hope these three methods help you overcome stress. Trauma will be the subject of the next section.

5.2 Stoic Ways of Getting Out of Trauma

Stoicism notes that, in order to thrive, we need only to restore our character to nature again, rather than to stay prisoner to the distortions absorbed from stressful events, as well as by society and culture. Our approach to trauma distorts our identity, such that it is no longer in accordance with nature. This suggests that we are not able to be normal or function normally.

Stoicism claims that by keeping our character according to nature, we thrive. The character may discern good from bad and behave accordingly. Nature would teach us if we would just look, how to discern, and behave. Note how distinct this teaching is from that of the popular culture of all ages, which claims that outward objects can make us prosper, such as possessions and humans. Stoicism maintains that external objects, unless we use them to create a character, do not help us thrive.

The fact that external things will help us prosper is one of the major fallacies of our civilization. Remember all the ads that every day bombard us. But, above all, trauma survivors know that money or land does not make us happy. It is better to have them, but they do not make us happy because we are still within our broken self at the end of the day, and we live with our constraints.

We need to restore our character in harmony with nature in order to prosper. If we use them to restore our character, external things may be beneficial. An important contributing factor to our struggle to succeed is that we have trouble differentiating between good and bad. Our responses to stressful experiences distort our processes of reasoning so that we contend with what is positive and what is evil. This happens on top of the regular distortions that society and culture present to us.

Stoicism claims that only goodness, virtuous acts, and moral excellence are "good." Vice versa (immorality) and acts driven by vice are the only "bad." "Neither good nor bad, something external" is "indifferent." It hinges on our actions.

Note the contrast between the Stoic and other societies' thoughts. The moral world is categorized by most societies into two categories: good and bad. It is divided into good and poor plus "indifferent" by Stoicism. I have described this before. Now let's discuss it in accordance with trauma.

Even before we came across trauma, our dualistic culture showed us an unconstructive way of thinking about good and bad. Society says that some external factors are good, such as income or families, and those other external things, such as poverty or low social status, are poor.

Stoicism, however, asserts that moral excellence is the only good thing and immorality is the only bad thing. And the rest is neutral. Chocolate fudge sundaes, while they are not calorically neutral, are socially neutral! Those thoughts and acts turn evil, not the chocolate or the fudge, or the ice cream shop if you cannot stop dreaming about them and buy one every day after work.

Note carefully that Stoicism means that we are inner of good and bad: it falls into our character; external objects are neutral, implying that they are not good or evil, but simply indifferent.

This tiny difference has enormous repercussions. Let's just discuss it.

We are conditioned by culture to separate external things into positive or evil (in total contrast to the state of nature). Stoicism, though, notes that they are neutral. Both external objects are oblivious to you, neither good nor evil. Wealth is not good or evil, either. Poverty is neither evil nor good. Neither good nor evil is family. Death is neither evil nor good. It is a normal phase.

Stoicism suggests that only "preferred" or "dispreferred" are certain external, indifferent items. They are "preferred indifferent," health, money, friends, families, etc. These are not "good;" they are the items to which our virtuous acts (or vice) are directed. "Dispreferred indifferent" are the things such as disease, hunger, death, alienation from society, etc. Sickness is not bad: it is an occurrence of good or sin to which we direct.

For trauma patients, this sort of thought has consequences.

Is it bad / evil, then, that you have PTSD (Post Traumatic Stress Disorder)? Stoicism says no; this is a morally neutral, despised experience, to which either goodness (good thoughts and actions) or sin (bad thoughts and actions) may be guided. As a human phenomenon, PTSD is an external, neutral thing: if you do not allow it, it will not affect your character.

I hope you understand now that you have to conquer the guilt to be able to see PTSD and the incidents that led to it as neutral things that are simply disliked. The next section will be about living a peaceful life without fear.

5.3 Stoic Ways of Getting out of Fear

It is a timeless fact that a lot of the things we are concerned about never happen. Yet our imagined fears may have actual repercussions. Fear will distort your reality and will distort your perception and confuse what is actually going on, like other intense emotions such as rage. Fear's grasp can be paralyzing.

How can you get the control back? How do you get back to your successful self-ready to face the obstacle that comes next?

First of all, one of the most important rituals of the Stoic tradition must begin: the pre-meditation. What is the worst thing that could go wrong? Study it. Feel it in the skin and bones. Understand what it is going to sound like and taste. When you are done, you will have lost the suspense and some of the fear. You have gotten yourself comfortable for the worst. The man who has expected the coming of trouble, as Seneca put it best, takes away their strength as they arrive.

Now prepare yourself. What will you do to brace yourself? When the worst-case emerges, what choices do you have? How do you prevent the existence of it? To reduce the likelihood of the worse happening, what will you do today?

How would you bounce back if it happens? On paper, write it all down and work about it. These moves are the main instruments in the "fear environment" exercise of bestselling author and entrepreneur Tim Ferriss, inspired by Stoicism, clarified your worries, imagining the worst-case scenario, coming up with ideas, and strategizing to avoid anything that might come.

Think of Cato, one of the worlds' most leading stoics, wandering about barefoot and in scant clothes in hot and cold. About why? For a life in which he would have to endure hardship, he was educating himself. He was a Roman aristocrat, of course; he would certainly never have been penniless. But he did not want to dread it at all, so he led a penniless life, in brief intervals. And that basic exercise gave him an unusual strength, the opportunity to experience and plan for and learn about a dilemma that stripped him of all his strength.

Military men know how to shoot to kill, but why are they preparing to be on the gunfire's receiving end? The same explanation that a corporation is doing "war gaming" against its rivals. Football players perform fumble recovery for the same purpose of giving reps to their replacement quarterback. You will reduce your fear when you can research and learn about what has failed in the past or brace for what may fail in the future.

Night and day, firefighters prepare to get into burning houses. Police officers fire hundreds of bullets at firing ranges to ensure that when a situation occurs, they are ready. Special operators around the world prepare for hostage rescue scenarios, carrying out the distant likelihood of an enemy catching one of our own over and over again.

Preparing for what may come is how you realize that you are able to enter a situation filled with confusion and turmoil. You have done your best to train. You take care of the fear in this way.

Think of practice as immunity to weakness; immunity to fear; immunity to your own, and hesitation and doubt. Practice what you do not think you can do, and you can discover you have more potential than you thought possible.

In brief, this is the blueprint that you require to take power over fear: In brief, this is the blueprint that you require to take power over fear:

1. Write down that. Just sense it.
2. Inquire if you can stop it.

3. Practice eliminates fear: do whatever is required to realize that for all your effort, you have steadied yourself and prepared.

Let me assert this strong conviction that fear itself is the only thing we have to fear. It is an irrational, nameless, unjustified dread that paralyzes required attempts to transform withdrawal into advance. The Stoics knew that, regardless of the suffering it caused, terror was to be hated. In contrast to the harm we do to ourselves and others as we unthinkingly scramble to stop them, the things we fear pale. An economic downturn is bad; turmoil is worse. Terror does not help a difficult situation; it just makes things worse.

The next section will be about controlling the biggest devil of all evil; anger.

5.4 Stoic Ways of Getting Out of Anger

If you learn how to let go of the rage, you will have conquered the wildest of feelings and will find it far easier to handle other states of mind. But even though you do not think you have a big rage problem, read on as you are going to discover more useful emotional intelligence insights. Marcus Aurelius tried notoriously to control his own temper. In his novel, he returns to this topic time and time again as he tells himself of different ideas that he has found useful in handling frustration. He also mentions stoic anger control tactics at one point. He explained them as "gifts from Apollo," meaning the healing deity. Five of them are here:

1. It is not the behavior that irritates you; it is your thoughts on it.

    This is one of Stoicism's most basic precepts and coping techniques. When it occurs in different situations or is handled by different persons, are you still similarly offended by the same behavior? Are other people similarly mad as they witness the kind of stuff that gets you upset? It is arguable because they have varying views and perceptions about the situation if there is any difference in the way people react. Ultimately, it is our moral assessments that decide how mad we are over something that reaches us in life. So, according to the Stoics, it is worth having that in mind and then asking whether we place too much emphasis on items within our direct control.

2. Mind that you are also not perfect.

The Stoics felt that acknowledging our own shortcomings was crucial for us. Stop and ask yourself if anyone offends you, if you may do certain things yourself, or at least have the ability to do things that others might find objectionable. As therapists tend to say, when you point a finger to accuse another person, you should remember the three fingers on the very same hand pointed in your own direction. Confessing that we are guilty of committing equivalent crimes to someone we are angry with will also alleviate our indignation, allowing us to think more rationally at the situation.

3. Your rage does more damage to you than what you are upset at.

This is a very common Stoic doctrine, too. Our traits are blurred by rage, which the Stoics claim appears grotesque and unnatural. However, it also distorts our brains by clouding our capacity to think. Anger is all transient insanity, they claim. The acts of other people only affect outward objects, our prestige, our possessions, or even our physical bodies, but our own wrath, according to the Stoics, ultimately hits deeper by harming our moral character. By stressing about what it costs us, we will also lose the grip rage on our minds: the detrimental effects of indulging in it.

4. Do not stoop to the level of them. React with compassion to rage.

The Stoics have sought to promote a better alternative way of looking at stuff, in addition to questioning their own feelings of frustration. Stoicism is simply an ideology that is really humane. Rage, according to them, is usually based on the conviction that something wrong has been done by others, and they deserve to be punished. The contrary will be the conviction that they need to be supported or may be informed. Marcus said that when he was upset by the aggressive actions of another human, after discussing his own feelings of rage, he would kindly take them aside and explain to them, without condescension, why they were only hurting themselves rather than him.

5. Accept the probability that they just do not understand why something is wrong.

The striking but divisive doctrine that no man intentionally does evil was taught by Socrates. Marcus states that when questioned, everyone excuses their actions; we all get upset if we are told that we are doing something morally wrong. Even Stalin and Hitler's monsters thought what they were doing was justified. In their own heads, criminals who know that what they are doing is wrong, always find reasons to justify that. Ancient thinkers rigorously discussed ethics with everyday people because they became very familiar with the ways in which we confused ourselves on what was right and wrong. Relatively uncertain about life, we are both. In a way to temper his frustration with people, Marcus tells himself of this.

The treasure of knowledge gifted to us by Marcus surely has the power to scare the evil of anger away. Next, we will talk about greed.

5.5 Stoic Ways of Getting Out of Greed

One of the darker elements in Roman history is the brutality of the mob. There was an angry crowd which, during the time of Marius, tore Saturninus to bits. The grieving, angry citizens, were there who, riled up by the funeral prayer of Mark Antony after Caesar's death, assassinated the poet Cinna just because he had the same name as one of the accomplices.

It is frightening what a group of people can do when civil society's unwritten rules break down. Perhaps there is no better day than Black Friday in America to think about this. Fresh off the gratefulness of Thanksgiving, by greedily gorging on stuff, we decide to reward ourselves.

A day whose entire purpose is in larger conflict with the Stoic concept of sympathy is difficult to think of. The same individuals who previously sat in a peaceful manner with their family are now ready to engage in hand-to-hand fighting over a flat-screen television deal. Instead of enjoying the time off, at lower and lower prices, individuals were lined up for hours in the cold season to buy more and more nonsense they did not actually need. Not to replace the nonsense they purchased last Black Friday, but to add to the stack. The only expense that Black Friday shoppers do not mind paying for those savings? Countless traffic accidents, yelling matches, and retail employees' collateral damage are trampled to death.

"What's bad for the hive is bad for the bee," as Marcus wrote in Meditations. It's difficult to argue that Black Friday is good for anything or anyone but the big business bottom line. So, it would be great if you spent this morning thinking about the larger picture, the biggest picture, instead of following the general public on a shopping spree and possibly a killing spree.

Since we are all human, all are part of the same greater body, and we should be humane to each other. We come from the same soil, and one day we will each return to it the same way. Not only does it affect other people because we forget this, it mourns many millions, but it still hurts us.

Marcus Aurelius teaches us to revere the gods and take care of one another. That is what sympathy is about. Oikeiôsis, love with your fellow human beings, is about that. We ought to live it every day, honestly, but today we ought to be particularly conscious of it.

As the exact opposite of the Black Friday sale, at Daily Stoic, we sell our Sympatheia coins at the full retail price before 6 a.m. on Monday, 2 December. But, if you purchase one, we are going to give you another one free of charge to give to a family member, friend, or colleague who might benefit from it.

As we launch the holiday season, as you struggle with demanding in-laws, travel delays, or queues, and long lines, we hope you have this idea in mind. Don't let you get infected with the new spirit of selfishness and materialism. Alternatively, we must all rely on assurances that we are not alone, that we are part of something greater than ourselves, that we all owe a responsibility to a greater good, over and above our own selfish needs and wishes.

All of us are interconnected and united and made for each other. The Stoics understood it. The Buddhists understood it, and so do we. Never can this reality be far from our heads.

5.6 Stoic Ways of Getting Out of Disabilities

The ancient philosophy of Stoicism is still massively crucial today, many western philosophers and health practitioners' claim.

The key to a calm mind lies in being honest about what we can and cannot control in our lives, according to the Stoics. Some aspects are actually out of our grasp, and when attempting to alter them, we cannot waste resources. We should plan to come into hard times and welcome them.

According to Stoicism, tragedy is all part of existence and is simply acknowledged instead of going on. That is really well, you would say, but what about those people out there who are still struggling, day after day? Those with debilitating illnesses, fear, injuries, sadness, and sorrow?

And when our children are the ones who suffer, it is much harder to make sense of it. As parents, protecting our children is our responsibility, and it is so challenging to see them face the daily struggles that their disabilities offer. The sadness we feel for them is very genuine, as is the remorse for the life they are supposed to have had. Is it not human and completely reasonable to grieve and to experience sorrow and sadness when our loved ones have experienced something very bad?

Yes, absolutely, in my experience. And getting stuck in this mentality is also very easy. 'It's not right; he did not deserve this. It should never have happened.' And to feel anger towards the racism and lack of acceptance that people display so much in the rest of the country. It is not shocking that parents feel so disconnected from certain special needs and that they and their children are 'hard-to-do' to meet all these difficulties.

It is enough to make one bitter for a lifetime, to remain in a constant state of bitterness and remorse, and to reflect endlessly on the injustice served by creation.

Can a stoic attitude be beneficial for parents of autistic children? Some of us are simply too drained to find solutions, strategies for coping; we simply work. It can feel like a miracle to only get through another day. We cannot help but think, 'what choice do we have when we are lauded for our strength and endurance, or even for how stoic we are? The Stoics taught, without bias or expectation, that we should see things as they are.

The Stoics taught, without bias or expectation, that we should see things as they are. This technique allows us to recognize what cannot be improved, to take steps when we can, and to press on to conquer our challenges with bravery and determination. When we are not overwhelmed by negative thoughts and judgments on how it should be, this is much better.

When applying to raise a child with disabilities is clearly not an easy philosophy. The truth remains that multiple challenges need to be addressed. It feels like an uphill fight and a relentless war all too much. It is really hard not to draw assumptions as to how things should have been.

Yet we do need a language to live by, instruments to help us make sense of it all and to help us manage the minefield while attempting to ensure that our own needs and our children's needs are fulfilled.

Stoicism does not mean that we should shake off our problems, and it does not mean that we should not experience our discomfort. More than that, we learn to let go of the bad aspects we cling to, tensions and resentment. To keep our thoughts organized and regulated so that with resilience and inner-stability, we can face those challenges. This is definitely something worth reaching for.

There appears to be a widespread myth that the grim and unemotional Stoics is. Sensing and overcoming thoughts is not the same as not experiencing them. So, for those out there who are facing a less common life, indeed, it is real that we have the work of a lifetime ahead of us. Perhaps we can begin to find more inner peace if we can continue to face the day-to-day struggles using the cardinal virtues alluded to by the Stoics (bravery, wisdom, and self-discipline, and morality.)

The practice of Stoicism may be particularly useful to those suffering from lifelong physical disabilities. The sense of a loss of physical agency may cause individuals to feel that they have lost all control over their lives. Stoicism may teach impaired people to accept their situation and recalibrate their life goals. Stoicism encourages one to think about what we can do instead of dwelling on what we do not do.

This was the stoic approach to stress, anger, greed, fear, trauma, and disabilities.

Chapter 6: Stoicism & Mindfulness

Life can be overbearing. Our heads are overflowed with chatter, our worldview is corrupted and skewed, and our capacity to be present is lost.

Sometimes, life is frantic and exhausting. And our happiness, health, schooling, jobs, and even the economy are influenced by it.

It is a world that is noisy. While keeping one eye on the children and another on the screen, you fold the laundry. When listening to the radio and driving to work, you prepare your day and then arrange your weekend. But you may find yourself losing your link to the present moment in a rush to complete necessary things, missing out on what you are doing and how you feel. Have you found whether this morning you feel well-rested or the forsythia is in bloom along your way to work?

There is increasing awareness that treatments focused on mindfulness provide treatment for our mental health. A somewhat less well-known fact is that our physical well-being is also greatly enhanced by these methods.

Mindfulness takes us beyond surviving and making do. The strategies allow one to see the world differently; to evolve, thrive, and live a more caring and fulfilling life.

Mindfulness is the process of keeping the attention on the current moment consciously and embracing it without judgment. Mindfulness is now being clinically studied and has been discovered to be a crucial factor in minimizing depression and enhancing general satisfaction.

To further emphasize the importance of mindfulness, here are a few benefits it carries:

- Growing your mindfulness potential encourages multiple attitudes that lead to a satisfying life. Being aware makes it possible to savor life's rewards as they unfold, lets you become actively involved in tasks and provides a better opportunity to cope with adverse events. Many people who practice mindfulness find that they are less likely to get wrapped up with worries about the future or remorse about the past by reflecting on the here and now, are less obsessed with worries about progress and self-esteem, and are more able to establish deep ties with others.

- Psychotherapists have turned to mindfulness therapy in recent years as a significant part of the treatment of a variety of topics, including drug abuse, depression, eating disorders, anxiety disorders, disputes between partners, and obsessive-compulsive behavior.

- If overall well-being is not enough of a motivation, scientists have shown that in a variety of ways, mindfulness strategies tend to enhance physical health. Mindfulness can help manage heart disease, alleviate stress, decrease blood pressure, improve sleep, decrease chronic pain, and alleviate stomach issues.

Now let's discuss where mindfulness comes into play in Stoicism.

Stoic Mindfulness

Buddhism and Stoicism have a lot in common while still possessing ample distinctions to give the practitioner, who is versed in one practice, pause for thought when meeting the other. Both Stoicism and Buddhism are strongly realistic philosophies with an emphasis on the here and now, especially in their more modern 'engaged' and non-renunciant types. Marcus Aurelius, the Roman Empire's emperor, whose private metaphysical diary the Meditations was saved, writes that only in this present moment does each man exist. Anything that has since been encountered or lies in confusion. One needs to be mindful that we are here right now that the present moment is the only moment to be alive. The advice given by Marcus Aurelius resonates with the Buddhist practitioner that your mind carefully focuses every hour on the success of the mission on hand, with human compassion, dignity, and liberty and benevolence, and puts all other thoughts aside. If you conduct each operation as if it were the last one, you will accomplish this.

It is not surprising, in this sense, that anything closely analogous to 'mindfulness' occupies a central position within Stoicism. It is called prosoche, which can be interpreted as 'attention' by Epictetus, the ex-slave whose lessons survive in a concise handbook Encheiridion and volumes of the Discourses. He teaches his students that prosoche is necessary for an ethical life and that even less evidently critical activities can be conducted with prosoche, such as singing or playing. Its implementations, indeed, are infinite. Is there some aspect of life that Prosoche does not apply to? 'The preservation of prosoche is an integral aspect of Stoicism.

In Stoicism, the meaning of developing a centered mind is reminiscent of the Buddha's assertion in the Dhammapada that not a father, not a mother, can help us better as much as a well-directed mind. It is inherently curious that something so close to mindfulness was key to what it took to be a Stoic.

'Prosoche' is concerned with fostering the potential for daily circumstances to apply core ethical precepts. The most critical one was to make sure that you rely on what you can do, not on what you cannot manage. And more specifically, in ways that suit a benevolent social being, concentrate on doing what you can manage. As long as the first factor is concerned, a crucial question that anyone who practices Stoic mindfulness would ask themselves will then be, "Where do I" put myself "in this situation?" Do I put myself in something that I cannot control, or do I put myself in something that I can control? If you 'put yourself' in the approval of your boss, something that is beyond your influence, so when she agrees, you will be content and deflated when she does not.

If you 'put yourself' in the approval of your boss, something that is beyond your influence, so when she agrees, you will be content and deflated when she does not. As a Stoic, you would treat the situation differently, thinking, what is up to me in this scenario? For e.g.,' up to you' will be to concentrate on doing my job well and calmly. Maintaining your relationship with your boss as much as possible from your side will also be "up to you." But other than that, there is nothing "up to you."

If you find that your emotions are 'investing' themselves in something you cannot manage, Epictetus told his pupils, remember to say to yourself, that is nothing to do with you. Only focus your attention on what you can do and do it well.

Let's have some ways to fulfill your spirit with stoic mindfulness.

- **Abandon Your Vanity**

  The first step to getting in touch with yourself is to be true to yourself. Shed the false beliefs about your being. Know who you are and have no shame of accepting it to flourish.

  Epictetus was born a slave; he lived in Rome, was then exiled, and spent the remainder of his time in Greece. He said it is difficult for a person to understand what he already feels he knows.

  If you want to follow the philosophy and, thus, any matter of interest to you, before you start, you must throw away conceit and unnecessary pride. Be willing to understand, be willing to set your pride behind ad to be willing to listen to the wisdom of others, and accept the pleasure of ignorance to understand, flourish, and create.

There is a Socratic irony, like "I know I do not know nothing."

The definition of modesty is the feeling or mentality that makes you better than anyone or possessing a lack of pride that you have no special value. Humility seems like a bad trait at first sight, more like a sign of vulnerability rather than power. In fact, humility is a form of modesty that, as an individual, a contender, and a leader, will get you very far in your life. Let's take another way at it. An individual is arrogant who lacks modesty. It is a person who just cares about himself and sees himself as better and better than others. As they do not understand their shortcomings, there is no place for an arrogant person to better themselves. An individual who is not humble does not have a mentality for progress. The world's greatest teachers continue to make mistakes. The best teacher in the world also has plenty to learn about the world, and as not only a trainer but also a pupil, they should always perform their duties. You would never be able to achieve your full potential if you do not grab the opportunity to see your own flaws. Life is a never-ending road of development and learning. Pride deprives a person of their capacity to accomplish.

For self-improvement, modesty is an asset. You consider the aspects of your life that require attention while leading a modest life. If your teacher proposes to adjust a method to help your ring results, you need to understand that your current technique might not be ideally tailored to your goals. That comes with letting the preconceived concepts go and trusting the teacher. You should allow these experiences to fuel your development and learning only with modesty and emotional intelligence.

- **Shorten Your Expectations**

Be mindful of the world. Be able to distinguish what is achievable and what is not. Most of us are torn by the duality between what is happening in our heads and what is really happening around us.

All of us have such assumptions that things can go in a particular direction. It carries set expectations for some of us that our relationships should be just as we have imagined: ideal spouse, relatives, children, and friends. For some, it is the hope that by now we should have it all worked out, that our careers should follow a carefully planned path, or that any special occasion should live up to the hype: birthday, engagement, or holiday abroad.

The problem with this line of reasoning is that higher aspirations are not equal to higher satisfaction, appreciation, or success ratings. In comparison, projecting set goals is in profound contrast to life-defining impermanence and uncertainty. To deny the fabric of life is to demand things to go towards a predetermined direction. No matter how hard you try, you will not and cannot erase all the confusion from your life.

There is no such thing as the way it should be, in fact. It is all in a state of continuous motion. The more you try to eradicate doubt and complexity from life, the narrower your comfort zone's confines get. True ease is discovered by accepting pain, not defending oneself from uncertainty, and this is the comfort paradox. The broader the spectrum of future situations you have prepared yourself to contend with, the better things can work out.

It is not that expectations are risky necessarily. Yet they become precisely that as we rely on a particular result beyond what the Stoics viewed as our 'reasoned decision,' one about which we have little to no power. Positive visualization is not so much a tactic as it is a blueprint for disappointment, putting hopes sky-high and focusing solely on the best-case situation. You will end up ruined sooner or later by someone outside your influence.

Expectations leave you weak, static, and reactive outside of your rational decision. It is limiting and inefficient to spend your scarce resources on attempting to control any variable and going from A to B as you have imagined it in your mind. It restricts what you are going to do, what you can do, and the person you are going to be.

And who is invincible then? The one that will not be distracted by anything beyond their reasoned choice.

A much more powerful strategy provided by the Stoics is pessimistic visualization, considering the spectrum of future effects, even the adverse and worst-case. The best minds do not sit around dreaming about an alternative, fanciful reality where everything plays out according to schedule. To navigate unavoidable hurdles and turn them to their benefit, they build resourcefulness.

The only worth-holding assumption is that you take advantage of chances to behave in compliance with your own beliefs and ideals. You should hope, regardless of present conditions or challenges, to harness your own resourcefulness and endurance to strengthen yourself. Build a momentum of your own.

It all boils down to the outlook. Prepare yourself to manage a variety of possible consequences, gain trust in that capacity, and restrict your assumptions beyond your reasoned preference. You rob failures and external events of their ability to catch you off balance and dictate your life as you follow this attitude.

Resilience rewards truth. It blinds you to anything except the one-track, imagined road you've expected by projecting predetermined goals of life. The mediation between truth and desires is at the base of both of these Stoic teachings.

Recognizing this inner war helps you to close the divide and continue to cultivate the mindfulness, discipline, and endurance it requires to make your own positive change. Otherwise, the only life you have is at risk of being detached and unhappy.

- **Moderation Approach**

Being mindful requires you to understand the correct ratio of everything you do. Know the limits. Know the boundaries.

As a society, we are proud of being extremes. We flaunt how we manage a few hours of sleep, how insatiable we are in our professions, and how luxurious our lives are due to an abundance of expensive goods. But the concern is that we still run the risk of taking our virtues too far as we strive to extremes, which crumble into their reverse, crushing character defects.

Qualities and virtues are not just something you do or something you do not have. Varying degrees of severity exist. In this case, a dualistic mindset proves risky when two categories struggle to capture the complexity that distinguishes existence. The tendency to label personal attributes as positive or poor and no in-between should be ignored.

Instead, using Aristotle's 'golden mean,' it is much more reliable to frame virtues in the sense of a continuum, which explains that the range of goodness is squarely located in the center, between abundance and deficiency. Seneca gives a related viewpoint as he observes that so-called pleasures, when they go past a certain point, are actually punishments.

The premise is that we see those on one end of the continuum who neglect a certain attribute and view it as a defect. Yet virtues are just as prominent indicators of failure in their abundance. In fact, you can be too competitive (insatiable), too caring (co-dependent), and too disciplined (repressed). In the delicate spectrum of virtue, only those that represent balance can identify this golden mean, shield themselves from the downside of the extremes, and create an equilibrium.

Let me help you understand:

1. **Between Being Lazy and Being Insatiable Lies Ambition:** Laziness is an enemy that is evident and a symptom of vulnerability. But in the other direction, the continuum extends further than ambition. A virtue is a measured ambition. It is important to have ambitions, goals, and a purpose towards which you are working. Yet we cross into the domain of insatiability when taken too far.

    This is where we burn out, unable to reconcile with the moment, and understand what we have in our lives already. Insatiability, in equal relation to laziness, is a defect. Retaining personal well-being becomes an impossible challenge without moderation of our goals.

2. **Between Being Fragile and Being Depleted Lies Endurance:** Among top performers, endurance is a common virtue. It is interchangeable with emotional and physical stamina in this sense. Many who lack the stamina to conquer the challenges of life are weak and will not exhibit the persistence necessary to set themselves apart. On the other

hand, though, there is a breaking point, utter fatigue, where you have nothing to offer.

Building resilience is critical. But know the breaking point in the training and guard yourself against burnout. You have got a restricted amount of energy. Only things that fall in line with your professional goals and priorities should be delegated with that energy. Do not crash into the dirt yourself.

3. **Between Being Cold and Being Co-Dependent Lies Empathy:** Empathy is more advantageous than indifference or coldness. The stronger and healthier your relationships will be, the more you will be able to handle specific circumstances if you are in tune with those around you. If left unchecked, though, empathy will contribute to codependence and derive your self-worth from satisfying others' emotional needs while neglecting your own.

Holding these extremes in mind is necessary so that you can use them as a checkpoint to work within the spectrum of morality. Check yourself, but still, make an attempt to distance yourself from such relationships if you find yourself in circumstances where people misuse your empathetic disposition.

- **Being Your Best Self**

Stoic Mindfulness is all about understanding yourself and then being the best possible version of yourself. Understand your flaws and do your best to polish your character.

Here are a few things which will help you be your best self:

1. **Finding Inspiration:** There is an explanation of why Marcus Aurelius' meditations begin with him, giving thanks to all those who played a part in his character's growth. Now, not all of us have the luxury of being surrounded socially by individuals who are a daily source of motivation for us. But fortunately, we live in a period where, at our fingertips, the wisdom of the best people ever to live is available. All we have to do is to look for them and learn all about what it

means to live with justice, with intent, with strength, with bravery, and with joy.

2. **Reading:** The single biggest shortcut to learning about the persons we aspire to imitate is by learning to read. Perhaps it is the shortest road to changing oneself. Particularly today, where access to almost all of the world's information is available at our fingertips, some of it dating back to potentially millions of years before our creation. It acts as a reminder of our own ephemeral nature and that it is so important not to waste all of the short time on this planet that we have.

3. **Being Virtuous:** The Stoics concluded that our desire to become our best self lies in direct relation to how much the four main foundations of virtue are followed—wisdom, boldness, justice, and temperance. We should be assured that no matter what happens, we can be prepared to benefit from anything that happens to us by making the acquisition of knowledge one of our key goals in a given year. We will face each of these scenarios with determination and never give up by exercising bravery, no matter

how challenging they can appear. We will protect ourselves from giving into excess by exercising temperance and never let our feelings get the best of us when it is most necessary. And we will know from practicing justice that no matter what the result of our cases is, we really wanted to do the right thing.

4. **Saving Time:** The remorse that accumulates as the years go on is one of the hardest things about not sticking to our resolutions. Then we get to the end of our lives and remember how much time we have lost, how much time we have been losing in our own ways. All the times we give in to frustration when it was within our control not to, and how much this has a negative effect on our lives, we know.

5. **Building Resilience:** The only big determinant of our fate lies in how we react to what happens to us. Not in the stuff itself. Think of the ones you most respect, those who have faced immense challenges and made them happier and stronger. Do not let your first instinct be to get off the path if anything negative occurs. Let this be a chance to learn and to bring out of

yourself the brightest. The more you overcome adversity, the better you become.

6. **Being Practical:** The goal of learning Stoic philosophy is to enrich the way we live our lives with any other facet. Stoicism is probably the most realistic of all philosophies, after all. It is not about arguing whether there is such a thing as free will or other complex universe philosophies, but about encouraging us to transcend negative feelings and act on what should be achieved. It is meant to keep us calm under pressure and to concentrate on our values. But there is no point in reading the letters of Seneca if we are not going to add them to our own lives immediately. Marcus Aurelius noted in the above quotation that in order to become the best version of ourselves, there just are not that many things we have to practice. It is possible to understand these things through thought, but can completely comprehend them through experience. When you do exactly that in the most stressful circumstances, you do not fully understand the strength of letting go of your rage. When you see how much peace it

would offer you to do so. All of this makes you more and more powerful and ready to survive the future challenges to which we will eventually be exposed.

- **Being Sincere**

As described above, be mindful of what you can control and what you cannot. Obsessing over things that are not in your control will only leave you hurt. Be sincere in what you do, and do not be greedy about the results.

For example, there is an example of a performer with stage-fright, and it is provided by Epictetus. He said to himself when he saw a man in anxiety, what could this fellow want? For if he did not want anything outside his grasp, how could he be anxious? That is why he displays little discomfort when performing on his own but does so as he reaches the theatre, even though he has a wonderful voice. Since he does not only want to sing well but to win applause as well, and that is no longer in his influence. Oh, why is that? Why he actually does not know what an audience is, or the crowd's applause. That is why he trembles and becomes pale. The singer's desire is to want the audience to cheer him.

When he does, he leaves all puffed up. By comparison, the Stoic singer insists solely on the success of his craft and does that well. If the audience applauds, he will be pleased, but that has never been the point of his singing. For making a presentation or voice, the same may happen. The irony, of course, is that the one who insists on his artwork, on being in the field, is more likely to do his or her job well and to win the crowd's applause. In brief, a simple practice of Stoic mindfulness may be to question yourself during the day at numerous points: why am I putting myself in this situation?

These are the few ways you can truly live your life to the most with stoic mindfulness.

Chapter 7 – Turn Yourself into a Better Person

My advice to you, as this is the last chapter of the book, is to maintain your focus on being a better person, and you can do that through Stoicism. We have got countless things to attend to on a daily basis. We have got emails to reply to and calls to make. There are meetings. The people we met yesterday are waiting for a response or a decision we promised we would make. Facebook beckons. And so do our dreams and our aspirations.

And still, no matter how many directions we find ourselves in, it is fair to say that Marcus Aurelius was under much greater stress. Make no mistake: a calm, peaceful place was not the ancient world. Crises and distractions, rumors, and optimistic goal-setting filled it, too. In the past, all the temptations we faced now have their analogies, plus situations were scarier, deadlier, and precarious.

Let's discuss the stoic approach to staying focused.

7.1 Sharpen Your Focus – The Stoic Way

We should listen to the order that Marcus gave himself when he was struggling to stay focused after one of those trying days. He said that focus on doing what is in front of you with strictly and with sincere seriousness, tenderly, happily, with justice.

And he was not just chiding himself for doing something unthinkable. There was a process, he said, for this concentration. Do it all as if it was the last thing you did in your life. That is Memento Mori's power. The key, Marcus said, was not to let your impulses override your mind and offer a clear reason to yourself. Aimlessness is a diversion enabler.

You have got the ability to concentration like a Roman. You should handle everything correctly. And you can, most importantly. Because that might well be the last act of your life that you do. Below are a few stoic ways to deal with lack of concentration towards your goals in life:

- **Doing Less**

  Do less if you want tranquility. Do what is crucial. Do less and do it well. Since it is not important to any of what we do or say. You would get more tranquility if you can remove it. But we still need to eliminate unnecessary expectations in order to eliminate the behavior taken.

We are so focused now on doing more things that we are losing sight of what is really important. What is worst, we are trying to achieve everything that is impractical, and we wind up going nowhere. Our to-do list is so big that we actually get off on hitting it all off.

For this purpose, Pareto's 80/20 theory can be used. The aim is to commit resources to the most relevant 2-3 activities that are expected to earn us higher returns.

So, look at your work list and ask yourself these questions:

1. What is the optimal result if I complete this assignment? This will help you in thinking about the returns.
2. How can I automate this task? It will help you concentrate your resources on items that really need your energy, leaving the rest to computers.

3. How can this assignment benefit me or anyone else? It will help you pull items out that are not likely to benefit anyone.

It is excellent to see more work get done. But, it is quite possible that the quality of the job will also be poor. Instead, consider the fact that we have a limited span of focus and reflect on sorting out two-three of the day's most important things and devoting the undivided attention to completing them.

- **Identify Control**

The key challenge in life is precisely is to classify and differentiate problems so that you can reassure yourself plainly that they are external, not under your influence, and that they have to do with the decision that you really influence. Where do you look for the good and for bad, then? Not to uncontrollable externals, but to the decisions that are your own inside you.

You would have found something if you visualized the process of a task — sometimes, not every stage of the process is within your influence. Working alongside others is a required skill in the new workplace. And it makes sense, to some degree, why we cannot do everything on our own.

Now, although partnering with others is fantastic for the organization's general benefit, it could leave us a little stuck on our road to productivity.

So, what can be done when we work for teams, and not everything is in our control? We can discriminate easily between actions that are in our hands and actions that are not.

The Stoics accepted the fact that not everything is beyond our influence in our lives. And therefore, it is not only irrational to get angry over these uncontrollable actions, but it can also drive us crazy. There will be no amount of complaining about your co-worker that will help them do their work. The fact of the matter is — we cannot influence the decisions and actions of other people.

Yet, we are able to monitor our job completely. To know that a certain part of the process is under our power, we should get clarification and leave the rest to others. And do our jobs.

- **Visualizing the Process**

Often, when we begin working on something, we fail to think about the process clearly. We only start with aspirations that are unreasonable. And this absence of clarification contributes to procrastination.

A blueprint for disaster that is all it is.

Applying logic to the tasks we do will mean gradually breaking down each task into discrete phases from the beginning until the process is visualized at the end. This will help us better identify how projects pass from one point to another and whether there are any obvious bottlenecks in the process, as well. This exercise will allow us to see the appropriate individual steps, allowing us a more practical understanding of what we can do with a hundred percent concentration today.

Mind Maps are valuable guides that will help us break down the method and see clearly the steps taken to execute a mission.

So, break down the three most significant activities for the day that you intend to achieve. Ask yourself about the desired outcome and, step by step, list the procedure. Focus then, with undivided attention, on one move at a time.

That is a formula for deep work.

Additionally, you will find that every single move is necessary once you disintegrate something into its individual pieces. In fact, however, work does not have a character. There is no "grunt work' in existence. There is a purpose behind every step that leads to something bigger.

- **Defining Success**

We are all well mindful of the fact that success is reliant on many factors. Some, in our power, whereas others, not quite. Our commitment is included under our total command, while external factors include items such as luck and the efforts of other individuals (in the case of a team task). And still, despite realizing this, failure at anything drives us off.

To the Stoics, pleasure meant doing their work. And the same philosophy, to some degree, may be attributed to success. Success is not meant to be whether or not we have done anything. Instead, the amount of work we put into a project should be determined by it. It needs to be the degree to which we have done our work.

Not only does this perception take complete hold over us, but it also allows us to focus when things do not turn out. And if there is anything we believe about reflection, it is that it makes us smarter.

So, calculate your success by your commitment the next time you focus on something. You have won, as long as you put your 100 percent into it. That is success. The results are external. Your efforts are internal.

By following the above four methods to sharpen your focus, you can make yourself more successful. Below we will discuss the three aspects of stoic philosophy to live a life of harmony and bliss.

7.2 Employ Disciplines of Stoicism – Key to a Harmonious Life

A very detailed study of the meditations of Marcus Aurelius called The Inner Citadel was published by the French intellectual Pierre Hadot, in which he discusses the Three Disciplines in-depth, using them as a basis for his exposition.

If we pursue the reading of Hadot, it simply gives a fairly straightforward and basic model for interpreting Stoicism's teachings. Traditionally, the way of Stoic philosophy was described as living according to nature or living harmoniously, and Hadot implies that all three disciplines are built to help us live in peace in various ways and that they join together to provide the secret of a harmonious and a serene way of life, practical philosophy as the discipline of living wisely. Here are the three stoic disciplines:

- **The Discipline of Assent**

  The discipline of "assent", according to Hadot, is the extension of the Stoic metaphysical subject of "logic" to everyday life. In reality, stoic "logic" contains components of what we would now label "epistemology." or "psychology." According to this view, the discipline of the agreement is the virtue of living as human beings in harmony with our own intrinsic essence, which entails living with both our thoughts and words with conformity with reason and truthfulness. It is tempting to see this practice as especially synonymous with "wisdom" or truthfulness as the cardinal Stoic virtue. Hadot calls the "inner citadel" the aim of this discipline because it requires constant knowledge of the actual self, the part of the mind responsible for reasoning and behavior, the chief good of life, where our independence and morality remain. According to the study of Hadot, while the Stoics usually refer to "judgment," they are mainly interested in tracking and analyzing their own implied value judgments. This forms the foundation of our acts, impulses, and feelings, in particular the irrational urges and vices that the Stoics were seeking to resolve. Stoics are to note the early-warning signals of disturbing or unhealthy impressions by constantly observing their judgments and taking a step back from them, maintaining their "assent" or consent, rather than getting "carried away" into unreasonable and unhealthy passions and vices. This prosochê, or "attention," is named by the Stoics to the governing faculties of the mind, to our decisions and acts.

- **The Discipline of Action**

According to Hadot, the action discipline "hormê", which means the beginning or original" impulse "to action) is the implementation of the Stoic metaphysical subject of" ethics "to everyday life. Stoic "ethics" require the concept of positive, evil, and indifferent things. The goal of life is often dealt with as "happiness" or satisfaction (eudaimonia). It requires the concept (righteousness, wisdom, self-discipline, and bravery) of the cardinal Stoic virtues. According to the fundamental doctrine of Stoicism, for good living and satisfaction, goodness is the only true good and necessary in itself. Stoic ethics also include the vices, resisting morality, and the "passions" that are unreasonable and pathological, defined as craving, anxiety, physical distress, and pathological or deceptive pleasures. According to Hadot, the discipline of behavior is basically the practice of living in peace with all humanity, which implies benevolently wishing all humanity to prosper and fulfill the purpose of life with satisfaction. Nevertheless, since the well-being of other persons is beyond our immediate jurisdiction, we must still wish them well in compliance with the Stoic "reserve clause" (hupexairesis), which literally implies inserting the caveat: "Fate allowing" or "God willing." This is one way in which robust behavior with emotional recognition is reconciled by the spiritual approach towards life. In other terms, Stoics do their best to behave with virtue while acknowledging in a rather distant way, whether success or loss, the product of their acts. In addition, Stoics would function on the basis of their objective estimation on which external consequences should necessarily be desired. Marcus Aurelius thus seems to refer to three clauses which Stoics should be constantly mindful of adding to, all their actions the following:

1. A reserve clause (hupexairesis)
2. Collective good (koinônikai)
3. Sensitivity to value (kat' axian)

It is tempting to see this discipline as specially related to the cardinal virtue of "justice," which the Stoics described as including equality and benevolence towards others. Hadot calls this discipline "action in the service of humanity" because, by a mechanism known as "appropriation" (oikeiosis) or expanding the circle of our inherent "self-love" to encompass all humanity, it means extending the same natural affection or concern that we are born experiencing for our own bodies and physical well-being to include the mental and physical well-being of all mankind.

- **The Discipline of Desire**

The discipline of "desire" (orexis) is, according to Hadot, the application of the Stoic metaphysical subject of "physics" to everyday life, which involves the Stoic study of cosmology, natural philosophy, and theology. According to this view, the discipline of desire is a practice of living in accordance with the essence of the world as a whole, or with Zeus or Deity in the language of Stoic theology. This includes taking a "philosophical approach" as necessary and natural for existence and recognition of our destiny. The cardinal virtues synonymous with self-control over excessive desires, which are "courage" or endurance in the face of fear and pain and "self-discipline" (temperance) or the capacity to renounce temptation and abstain from deceptive or harmful pleasures, are especially enticing to see this discipline as involving. Hadot names this discipline's goal "Amor fati," or the caring embrace of one's destiny. One of the most compelling passages from the Enchiridion sums up this discipline that does not look for events to happen as you like, but for events to happen as they do and your life will proceed serenely and smoothly. The Stoic soldier Cato of Utica famously marched through the deserts of Africa through the broken remains of the Republican army to make a dramatic last defense against the tyrant Julius Caesar, who attempted to topple the Republic and proclaim himself Rome's emperor. He became a Roman hero even after he lost the civil war, and the Stoics called him "the mighty Cato" because his will was absolutely unconquered-he ripped his own heart out with his bare hands instead of submitting to Caesar and being used for his propaganda by the tyrant. Centuries later, despite a crippling plague and numerous misfortunes beyond his grasp, the Stoic emperor Marcus Aurelius repeatedly led his depleted army into battle to protect Rome from invading barbarian hordes. Regardless of the many challenges to conquest, he won. Rome would have been lost if he had failed.

These are three disciplines action, assent, and desire.

I have discussed the two factors which play into being your best self and living your best life in a serene manner. I would like to discuss two more aspects that play into living your life in the best possible way, and these are renouncing negative emotions and self-discipline.

7.3 Stop Fostering Negativity – Critical for a Positive Life

Stoic thought's objective is not to mitigate unpleasant emotions but to see the world as it is and foster virtue. Emotions matter because they hinder the universe from being viewed correctly. When we get caught up in them, it happens. When they move towards behaving without purpose, emotions count as bad.

The focus is not, from this viewpoint, on reducing negative emotions. The emphasis is on behaving with rationality and being committed to acting on our principles.

When one focuses one's mind on mitigating bad feelings, this dynamic will arise. Rumination may be driven by battling them. Rumination can give way to pessimistic thoughts. It continues the loop.

Imagine a pessimistic thought as a flame. A burning flame will not do any harm in an empty concrete parking lot. These flames are left on their own to die out or are quickly extinguished. In a locked space packed with combustible material, bring the blaze, and you have a possible tragedy on your side.

The fire would use any bit of flammable material in the space to burn hotter, longer, and stronger until it is quickly extinguished. .The single blaze left uninterrupted will become an uncontainable inferno that will burn until its flames have nothing left to feed on.

People feel a common scenario when they are a host to negativity. By the time it eventually runs its course, a person has been broken by all the rage, resentment, and blame from physical, emotional, and spiritual fatigue.

In a way, emotions are a tool. They are able to provide useful world knowledge and inspire us to behave well. When we get caught up in them and losing contact with reality, they get in the way. When we confuse feeling with how things are and when they influence us to behave in ways we would not reflectively support, feelings blind us.

The way to fix this is not to preclude bad thoughts from being encountered. We should embrace the bad emotions as they are. One may practice through typical stoic techniques, such as praemeditatio Malorum or by meditation,

Why does it matter? As the target distracts from what is really important, tension reduces negative emotions. Instead of staying out of one's mind and behaving with virtue, one's time can be expended battling toxic feelings. In comparison, working on reducing bad thoughts will make them worse.

I hope you have understood now how much negative emotions can put a strain on your life, and it is absolutely essential to break the negative cycle, so you do not faint running in circles from exhaustion. Let's move on to self-discipline.

7.4 Self-Discipline – Biggest Secret to a Fulfilling Life

Troubling moments make you feel as if the entire life is coming to a standstill. Life never fails to move and evolve. Time cures, and you are going to find yourself moving again, so you are going to have to do it in your own way. Difficulties are part of growth.

You can get better from a situation, but only if you have the right attitude. Some lessons may include: learning to let go of the past, being stronger, speaking more clearly, forgiving and rising, and putting faith in your gut. Life is a blessing; keep loving it, do not forget. We have little power over many of the external situations, but what we do have power over is the way we react. Existence is frail. Spend your time to enjoy life wisely. Life is intended to be experienced, to be felt and appreciated profoundly. Scientific analysis is demonstrating that it promotes cell development in the brain by taking on challenges. It encourages us to cope and to create resilience.

Discipline is the basic action, attitude, and ideology that holds a person in a routine and makes progress towards which he or she is following. Philosophy is not just about chatting or reading dense texts. It is something that people have used to accomplish their personal and professional accomplishments throughout history.

Our ego most frequently runs away from something that tells us of the fact that it is at odds with the cozy narrative we have made for ourselves. Any new pursuit is vital to its starting point. Stoicism doesn't make a difference. Stoicism is a practice we should use to become better friends, better in the profession, and better people overall. Without self-discipline, no personal progress, accomplishment, or goal can be realized. It is the most critical quality required for some sort of personal or technical excellence or excellent results to be attained. We also discover the hard way that external forces rule our universe. No phase takes place immediately, just as muscle building takes time, so self-discipline takes time to create. The more you practice and develop, the more you get stronger.

An integral feature of Stoic philosophy is self-discipline. Stoicism, not authoritarianism, is about self-discipline. We have actually no clue what other people are dealing with. The Stoics tell us because we have no idea what their inner world is like. We would not judge them if we did.

Through the mastery of our emotions, self-regulation begins. You cannot regulate what you do if you do not regulate what you say. Motivation keeps you moving; you keep rising with discipline. This is why we cannot let strangers decide whether or not anything is worth it. Within us is the secret to success.

These are the four aspects explained in Stoicism, which can lead you to be better as a human being.

I hope this book excited your minds about Stoicism, and you have grasped the fundamentals of this philosophy. The second part of this book is the practical version of this one. The detailed 30,000 words solely entail everyday practices and exercises for the modern stoics at home and also in the workplace so they can find real happiness. So if you want to live happily, which is something not very common and almost impossible in this chaotic world, you do need an understanding of Stoicism to help you achieve that. Stoicism teaches you that in reality, it is not the world around you, which is chaotic; it is our mind which is chaotic. Peace comes from within.

Conclusion

You have the authority to build the life that you desire. Learning how to become emotionally strong is an important ability that can help you get there. This book is a chance at life for people who lack emotional stability. The good news is that mental power is like a muscle: the more you use it, the better it gets. That would put an end to a continuous cycle of procrastinating your goals, big or small, and finally, bring the discipline to your life that would lead you to live a fulfilling life. You would not let others bring you down either by their words or actions. You would not stop believing in yourself, and you will never be a victim of circumstance. You would stand strong in the face of adversities. You would finally understand that you have control over your reactions to external factors, and that is a game-changer.

Emotional stability and all the good things in life come with stoicism. Stoicism is an ancient philosophy initially put forward by a rich merchant, Zeno of Citium, around 301 BC. The most prominent teaching of stoicism is to focus on the inside to prepare a sensible response to the outside and not letting the external events have control over your life. Important figures like Walt Whitman, George Washington,

Frederick the Great, Adam Smith, and many more have been found to study, admire, and follow stoicism.

The three prominent teachers of stoicism after Zeno were Seneca, Marcus Aurelius, and Epictetus. One was a roman emperor, and the other was a slave. This shows the diversity of the application of this philosophy. All three of them made significant contributions to the way of life that is stoicism. Most of the teachings of Seneca come in the form of letters. He wrote a collection of essays on diverse, realistic matters like adversity, mortality, frustration, tranquility, leisure, and happiness. Marcus wrote a book Meditations that is the authoritative book on personal integrity, self-discipline, modesty, power, and self-actualization. Epictetus wrote a handbook filled with stoic maxims and values, and there is a collection of discourses as an interaction between him and his students on topics like friendship, sickness, anxiety, hunger, tranquility, and why other people need not be upset with each other.

The first chapter serves an introductory purpose of the stoic philosophy. Stoicism has been manipulated as the emotionless philosophy of the ancient period, but what it truly is a powerful tool to bring your emotions and actions in a well-defined harmony. It got its name from Stoa Poikilê, a place for Zeno and his students to get together and celebrate the teachings of stoicism. There are four virtues in stoicism, namely justice, courage, temperance, and wisdom. These virtues are the fundamentals of the stoic philosophy, and there is still to date nothing more valuable in life than these four values, and there will never be anything more valuable too.

Stoicism stands on many core-beliefs like agreement with nature, focusing on the controllable, living by virtue, understanding the difference between good, bad and indifferent, taking action, loving the undesired, practicing misfortune, making opportunities, mindfulness, and many more.

The second chapter encompasses the journey of stoicism and covers the classical stoic period divided into three time zones. Stoicism has found a significant place among the modern generation as it revived because of three major reasons like the failure of social structures, massive information accessibility, and the undeniable nature of its advice. People who have made big names in the modern-day like Bill Gates, Elon Musk, Pete Carroll, and Warren Buffett, all owe their success to stoicism. The ancient philosophy offers solutions to many modern-day problems.

The third chapter deals with stoic practices that can still be applicable in the modern-day like stoic acceptance, time-saving, going beyond pleasure, embracing your distress, and strict honesty.

Chapter four is dedicated to building emotional resilience through practices like stoic meditation, avoiding impossible hope, accepting fate, Momento Mori (reminding yourself of death), Premeditatio Malorum (contemplating on the worst that could happen), accepting difficulties, responding to and turning hardships into opportunities for growth and eradicating ego.

Chapter five is comprised of dealing with anger, fear, greed, trauma, and stress in accordance with the stoic teachings like distinguishing pain from suffering, creating a gratitude list, understanding that you are not perfect, and many more.

The sixth chapter includes ways to nurture stoic mindfulness like abandoning vanity, shortening expectations, acquiring a moderate approach, and being your best self by finding inspiration, being sincere, being virtuous, and building resilience.

The final chapter of this book deals with being the best version of yourself. It can be done by sharpening your focus, acquiring the three disciplines of stoicism, i.e., action, assent, and desire, renouncing negative emotions, and maintaining self-discipline.

If there is one thing that I want you to take away from my book is to live in accordance with nature. If you are mindful of yourself, you will be able to better control how you respond to the happenings around you.

The second part of this book is fully equipped with daily routine exercises and practices. This book would not be just applicable in your personal life but also in your workplace so you can be happy in the truest sense. It is a detailed book of 30,000 solely devoted to the practical use of stoicism. Make sure you check it out as it can offer you the secrets of a peaceful and fulfilling life, which is getting harder and harder to achieve in the modern world.